THE INSIDER'S GUIDE TO

BOAT
CLEANING
AND
DETAILING

INTERNATIONAL MARINE / MCGRAW-HILL

Camden, Maine • New York • Chicago • San Francisco • Lisbon • London • Madrid
• Mexico City • Milan • New Delhi • San Juan • Seoul • Singapore • Sydney • Toronto

THE INSIDER'S GUIDE TO
BOAT
CLEANING
AND
DETAILING

*Professional Secrets to Make
Your Sailboat or Powerboat Shine*

NATALIE SEARS

Library of Congress Cataloging-in-Publication Data

Sears, Natalie.
    The insider's guide to boat cleaning and detailing : professional
secrets to make your sailboat or powerboat shine / Natalie Sears.
        p.   cm.
    Includes index.
    ISBN-13: 978-0-07-159693-0 (alk. paper)
    ISBN-10: 0-07-159693-3 (alk. paper)
    1. Boats and boating—Maintenance and repair.   I. Title.

    VM322.S437   2009
    623.82'020288—dc22   2008052161

1 2 3 4 5 6 7 8 9 10 11 12 13 14 15 16 17 18 19 20 21 22 23 24 25 26 27 28   DOC/DOC   0 9

ISBN   978-0-07-159693-0
MHID   0-07-159693-3

McGraw-Hill books are available at special quantity discounts to use as premiums and sales promotions or for use in corporate training programs. To contact a representative, please visit the Contact Us pages at www.mhprofessional.com.

This book is printed on acid-free paper.

To my grandfather Nick, who always taught me that I could do anything I put my mind to and couldn't possibly fail as long as I simply tried

CONTENTS

ACKNOWLEDGMENTS

I would like to express my deep gratitude to a few of the many people who helped me start and manage my boat-detailing company, without which I wouldn't have gained the experience that made it possible for me to write this book: To my sister Cherie, who held my hand as she walked me down to the dock that very first day and gave me the confidence I needed to help me take my business from idea to reality. To Dan, who supported me along the way both the first and second time around and encouraged me to go to college so I could be a boat washer with a business degree. To Lee, who has put in so many hours of hard work and helped take a huge load off my plate so I can have lunch with my sister almost daily, and who somehow puts up with me even during my most crazed moments at the boat shows. And to Bill King of Compass Point Yachts, who gave a new detailer a chance and helped my business grow over the years. I am truly thankful and grateful to all of you.

Not All Boats Are Broads

I know you're just dying to learn how to clean the bird droppings from your boat's foredeck, the mildew from its canvas, and the boatyard overspray from its hull. I know you're anxious to get started, but let's ease into this. There's a lot to learn if you haven't done this before or if you're looking for better, more effective techniques. There are tips and tricks sprinkled throughout each chapter that can ease the job of cleaning and detailing your boat and make the work more pleasant. There will be time for all of that, but first allow me to introduce myself and this book.

Why I Wrote This Book

I used to think it was fun to hang out in the boat-cleaning aisle of my local boating supply store and watch unsuspecting boaters stare with glazed expressions at the overwhelming array of products calling out to them from the floor-to-ceiling shelf displays. "No need to buff!" or "Lasts for seven years!" the cans and packaging proclaim—or my personal favorite, "Never need to wax your boat again!" Eventually I'd decide to help my fellow boaters, but more often than not, before I could swoop in to save the shopper from buying five products that don't work and suggest the one that does, a sales associate would spot his victim and saunter over. When I picture this scene, the associate is always a 17-year-old kid who has never cleaned a boat and is working there only because his dad wants the store's employee discount. "Oh yeah," the kid says. "That's my favorite product, and it works great on every type of boat and for every kind of stain. And it lasts for seven years."

That is why I wrote this book—to help you when you're standing in that aisle, and to go on helping you when you're aboard your boat, maintenance tools and supplies at the ready. I wrote it to share what I have learned from working in this industry all these years, and to pass along some helpful tips and tricks so you can learn from my experience rather than your own trials and errors. I wrote this book so you have the information you need at hand to care for your boat, whether it's new or used, whether it's your first boat or your tenth, whether you maintain your boat yourself or hire a detailer.

Rain Is What I Know

I live in the Pacific Northwest, so although I've included information about boat cleaning in any locale or climate, you may notice that my experience comes from what I know—gray skies, clean water, and lots of rain. Before researching this book, I had no idea that folks in Florida have to use water filters and softeners or that Southern California boaters don't have to cope with water streaks that reappear on an almost daily basis. Also, my experience is mostly with fiberglass boats. Most owners of wooden boats prefer to do their own work, so although I love wooden boats, I have not yet had enough experience with them to consider myself an expert.

You will encounter references to "Opening Day." Here in the Pacific Northwest we generally put our boats away for the winter because of the cooler temperatures, rough seas, and rainy days. Come March and April, the rain lets up (a little), and we all come out of hibernation to start preparing for boating season, which we joyously ring in on May 1—or, as we call it, Opening Day.

This Book Is Written for . . .

▶ New boat owners who have never previously owned a boat
▶ Veteran boat owners who have never maintained their boats but now want to start because the work looks enjoyable, or because there's no better way to get to know your boat than by working on it, or because they want to save money
▶ Boat owners who want to hire a detailer to do the work but need a manual to tell them what a detailer should or shouldn't do
▶ Owners of boat-detailing companies who want to provide employees with a guidebook

If you're already an expert professional boat detailer, you will see that I don't provide every last tip and trick. When you work in the industry long enough, you come across interesting fixes for almost every boat detailing conundrum, no matter how obscure. However, not all such fixes are appropriate for those who are less experienced with gelcoat properties, chemical reactions, or how to remedy the situation when they've accidentally confused the container of pink antifreeze for the container of pink boat soap. For a book like this one, the tried and tested basics are best. The techniques in these pages cover every common scenario and many uncommon ones, and you'll learn other shortcuts and secrets naturally along the way. (Here's one for you: Don't keep the pink antifreeze next to the pink boat soap. Not that we've ever done this before, of course. . . .)

In summary, this book lays a solid and safe groundwork for cleaning and detailing your boat. It is written above all for the boatowner who has to care for only one or maybe two boats, rather than the boat maintenance worker whose job is to care for seventy boats.

Not All Boats Are Broads

I'm not one of those people who refers to every boat as a "she" because I'm not completely convinced that all boats are of the female persuasion. I have met many a boat with sharply angled features that won't go in the right direction without sensible guidance and that seems to attract dirt. Such boats are obviously male. Likewise, I have met many a boat with beautiful curves and lines that is extremely stubborn when it comes to stain removal and that won't stop squeaking or creaking when worked on. Those boats are obviously female. So, at least until I learn a boat's personality, it remains an "it" to me.

Instructions Are for Others

I'm the type of person who thinks instructions are for others—which is probably why my cooking never turns out very well. You can be assured that I have not simply filled my chapters with rewritten instructions from cleaner, wax, and soap containers and called that good. That's because I've never really read those instructions—I've merely glanced at them and then figured out better ways to use the products. Just as you might change a recipe by adding your own favorite ingredients or cooking it differently, I use boat cleaning products in combination with my own preferred cleaning tools and techniques to achieve the results I'm looking for. You can have confidence in the instructions I give for using each product; however, if you're ever in doubt or don't have this book in front of you, the instructions on the back of the bottle won't let you down.

I hope you will enjoy this book, learn from it, and keep it as a practical reference guide for as long as your heart belongs to your boat.

THE INSIDER'S GUIDE TO
BOAT
CLEANING
AND
DETAILING

CHAPTER 1

Washing Your Boat

It's finally a beautiful spring day and you decide to head down to your boat to get the engines running or take it out for a spin. But what you see when you get there causes shock and awe. Your boat is heavily dusted with a brown layer of dirt. Footprints from your last outing of the previous year remain on the nonskid. Something slimy and green is oozing out of the rubrail. The gloss on your hull is missing. The gelcoat is covered with water stains. And worst of all, it looks like entire bird colonies have been dive-bombing your boat (and only your boat) all winter long.

A boat covered in mildew after a long winter's nap

Washing your boat—preferably on a regular basis—is an important task of boat ownership. It should be an enjoyable task, and I can assure you that when you have the right gear and products on hand and know exactly how to tackle this job, you'll find it peaceful and easy work. How many other ways can you think of to experience nature, fresh air, a peaceful environment, and healthy exercise while accomplishing useful work with results that are immediately and gratifyingly obvious?

This chapter covers the following topics:

▶ Why you should wash your boat
▶ How often to wash your boat
▶ Gear and supplies needed
▶ Preparation
▶ How and where to start
▶ Removing water streaks
▶ Treating mildew
▶ Washing the tender
▶ Keeping your boat clean on a regular basis

Why Wash Your Boat?

This seems like an easy question with an easy answer. Why wash your boat? To get it clean. But there's more to it than that, and more to it than meets the eye. To answer a question with another question, what will happen to your gelcoat if dirt, airborne particles, stains, and moisture are allowed to remain on it for long periods of time? The answer is that these agents start to break down the integrity of the gelcoat. A brand-new boat with a nice glossy finish can look dull and faded within a year if it isn't washed on a fairly regular basis. Of course, the best way to protect a gelcoat finish is to wax the boat once or twice a year (covered in the next chapter), but regular washings can help prolong the gelcoat's appearance and protection.

Small airborne particles of dirt land constantly on the hull and decks. Unless you wash your boat regularly to remove this layer of dirt, you are basically grinding it into nonskid deck surfaces and scratching the gelcoat with it as you walk around your boat and brush against the side of the house structure and elsewhere. Likewise, if your fenders or lines sit on or rub over any section of the gelcoat, they will grind in dirt particles and leave marks in those areas.

Bird and spider droppings, if not washed off regularly, will eventually stain the gelcoat. If your boat is docked near a tree, sap may fall onto the gelcoat, creating a sticky residue that attracts dirt and other particles. Any rainwater or moisture that does not bead off the gelcoat but instead remains standing on the finish will eventually cause mildew growth. Salt spray that remains on the gelcoat or windows will eventually etch into the finish, especially if the boat sits in direct sunlight. Over time, your once glossy gelcoat finish will fade, becoming lightly scratched in high-traffic areas and acquiring light brown stains from droppings that have soaked into the finish.

There are some maintenance tasks on a boat that, if left unattended to, will only cause expensive repairs in the future. I'm not going to go so far as to say that a failure to wash your boat on a regular basis will actually do any major damage. No boat will ever sink from too heavy a cargo of dirt, bird droppings, and oxidation. (Thank goodness!) If your boat is not washed on a regular basis, however, the cleaning you will eventually have to do to get the boat looking good again will become a much larger job than necessary. Further, once bird droppings or water stains have soaked into the gelcoat, a simple wash will no longer remove the stains. Your only option to remove the stains at this point is to wax your boat, which can be costly and time-consuming and require a lot of hard physical work.

Additionally, keeping your boat washed and detailed on a regular basis will definitely help its eventual resale value. A clean boat shows a prospective buyer that the owner cares about its appearance, and such an owner probably cares for the boat in other ways as well. A clean boat is likely to be a well-maintained boat, and a dirty boat is hardly ever well maintained. Boat brokers typically refuse to show a dirty boat and will request that you wash your boat or have it detailed before they'll show it to prospective buyers. If you are planning to sell your boat, read more about how to prepare it for sale in Appendix A, "Selling Your Boat."

How Often to Wash Your Boat

You should wash your boat or have it washed by a detailer at least once every couple of weeks, and hose it off with fresh water after any saltwater excursion. You can go longer between washes if you keep a good coat of wax on your boat or if you moor it in a covered slip. But if your boat is not in a covered slip, if you take it out often on salt water, or if you moor it in a wet location (for example, the Pacific Northwest), you should wash it every two to three weeks. Obviously, the more often you wash your boat, the better, provided you're using good products and supplies (covered in the next section) that won't strip the wax off the gelcoat. If you wash your boat regularly, it won't get so dirty that washing it becomes an odious task. After a certain point, dirty boats just get dirtier. Don't let your boat reach that point.

Gear and Supplies

If you've owned a boat for a long time, you probably have a dock box full of half used cleaning products you bought over the years that promised magical results. Now would be a good time to go through those products and throw out any that are almost empty or look old. Also throw out any cleaners in containers that have cracked, rusted, or ripped. You can be sure that the integrity of the cleaning product has deteriorated, and there's no reason to handle rusty cans or sharp edges. Take the Turtle Wax, dish soap, and any other auto or household cleaning products back to the garage, and find another use for any cleaning products that aren't biodegradable or meant specifically for marine use. You'll probably be left with an assortment of colorful boat soaps, cracking paste waxes, and spray products from companies who can't seem to spell correctly ("Brite" and "Klean") that promise to remove any stain that even thinks about coming near your boat. If your half-used boat-specific products are no more than two years old and have been properly sealed in containers that show no signs of wear and tear, consider them usable. A few household cleaners are useful on the exterior of a boat, and I mention those in this section, but they should be used sparingly and wiped on and wiped off (as opposed to being hosed off) if possible.

A Short Lesson on "Biodegradable"

Most of the boat cleaning and washing products you'll find at a boating supply store say "biodegradable" on them. This simply means that these products are capable of being decomposed by biological agents in the water, such as bacteria. A biodegradable product like boat soap will eventually "break down" in the water, whereas a nonbiodegradable product (such as oil) will remain in its current state or form. Still, biodegradable products can kill or sicken waterfowl and fish. This is because most soaps and other cleaning agents contain phosphates, which encourage excess plant growth.

While small amounts of phosphates constitute a beneficial nutrient (they encourage excess plant growth) and are necessary for photosynthesis, large amounts biodegrade slowly, and their effects are felt for a long time. Excess phosphates increase the acidity of the water and speed up the growth of algae. Algae in normal quantities is the essential base of the aquatic food chain, but algae blooms block light and choke water flow, making it difficult for other living organisms (both plants and fish) to exist in that environment. In essence, such blooms slowly suffocate the creatures living in the area. You might think an algae bloom, through photosynthesis, would increase the dissolved oxygen in the water, but in fact the opposite occurs. Dead and decaying plant material use up the available oxygen. Any marine organisms that can escape the area do so, and the rest die. This local catastrophe is familiar to anyone who has lived beside a eutrophic lake, but marine waters are not immune.

Soaps and Stain Removers

I'm the first to admit that the best soap for washing pretty much anything, including a boat, is good ole dish soap. Who doesn't appreciate all of those hardworking suds and a lemon-fresh scent? And it's tempting to use dish soap, because we all own plenty of it, it's easily portable, and a little goes a long way. But whatever you do, please don't wash your boat with dish soap . . . or Soft Scrub . . . or Ajax . . . or Windex. These products may be excellent choices for their intended uses, but not for washing a boat. Leave your household cleaners at home, or at least most of them. I list those that can be helpful in the appropriate section, but first here is a list of household cleaners that should *not* be used on your boat. All of these are in common use on boats, but none of them should be. The last column is a list of what to use instead, and I go into more detail on each of those products below.

Cleaning Activity	Household Product	Why Not to Use	Use Instead
Washing boat	Dish soap	Causes hazing and removes wax over time.	Boat soap
Removing marks or stains on gelcoat	Soft Scrub	Scratches gelcoat and removes wax.	Wax

continued

Cleaning Activity	Household Product	Why Not to Use	Use Instead
Cleaning nonskid or vinyl surfaces	Ajax or Soft Scrub	Leaves a powdery residue to clean up and can scratch vinyl finish.	Magic pad, Black Streak Remover
Cleaning windows	Windex	Streaks and causes hazing on Lexan.	Sprayway or Mer-maids
Removing stains on gelcoat	Fantastik or similar all-purpose cleaner	Contains harsh chemicals, causes yellowing of gelcoat, and removes wax.	Simple Green or Krazy Clean
Washing boat, cleaning stains	Car soap and spray cleaners	Meant for clear coat and might not be biodegradable.	Soap and spray cleaners from boat supply stores
Removing brown algae stains	Soft Scrub, rubbing compound	Too harsh on gelcoat.	Rust SprayAway (rust spray cleaner)
Removing mildew on gelcoat, canvas, or nonskid	Lysol or Tylex mildew remover spray	No reason—these work very well, but if you want to stick to a biodegradable product, use . . .	Mold-Off Mildew Cleaner

Let's talk about boat soap first, since that is the main product you'll use to maintain your boat's cosmetic appeal and keep it clean on a regular basis. All boat soaps on the market are required to be biodegradable, and most contain an agent that creates suds. Some contain wax. Many are pink. You shouldn't choose a soap by its color, but neither should you choose one by what the back of the bottle says it can do for your boat. They all help to get the dirt off your boat, but only because you're standing behind the deck brush moving it back and forth. None of them do the work for you. (I swear I have found a few brands of soap that actually say the soap will do all of the work. If that were the case, I'd squirt the soap all over my house, truck, and horse and then go have a seat and watch them get clean!)

I have tried boat soaps that cost $21 per gallon and boat soaps that cost $4.99 per gallon. The more expensive ones lasted longer as more water was added to the bucket, but that really benefits only a detailer washing seven boats in a row or an owner washing a boat that is 50 feet long or longer. The most expensive boat soap I've used smelled good and contained a light wax agent. The least expensive did a good job of removing dirt and most stains, also contained a wax, and maintained its suds long enough to be effective. I have also used soaps meant for automobiles, and they worked just as well and were often much less expensive than soaps marketed specifically for boats.

Boat soaps with wax don't actually add a coat of wax to the gelcoat. Your boat won't bead up or look more glossy than it did before you washed it. The purpose of waxing a boat is to remove oxidation and protect the gelcoat from harmful ultraviolet (UV) rays and other elements. The only way to remove oxidation is to cut through the top layer of gelcoat with a rubbing compound, preferably using a buffer, and no soap will

> *Note:* There are many different brands of boat soap and cleaners on the market. I live on the West Coast and am most familiar with the brands that are popular there. Usually I focus on what to look for in a particular product or piece of equipment rather than touting specific brands. Keep in mind that there are many specialized brands out there that may not even make it to the shelf of your local boat supply store yet might be superior to what is mass-marketed. As long as a product is meant for boats or gelcoat, is biodegradable, and doesn't contain drying agents such as alcohol or acetone, there's no reason not to give it a try for its intended purpose on your boat.

do that. The main benefit of a boat soap containing wax is that, at the very least, it won't strip any wax from the gelcoat (as a harsher soap such as dish soap would do), and at the very most it might add a thin layer of a UV-protecting agent to the gelcoat to slow the oxidation process. But don't depend on boat soap to stop oxidation in its tracks. That is the full-time job of a good coat of wax.

I have seen many boat owners use Soft Scrub to remove a stain or mark (such as bird or spider droppings, a scuff mark made by black-soled shoes, a grease or food stain, or water stains) from a section of smooth gelcoat. And why wouldn't they? This paste-like product does the job! But it also removes wax and can scratch gelcoat, thus making that section more susceptible to future staining and oxidation. From a cosmetic standpoint, if your boat is fairly glossy, any area you clean with Soft Scrub will stand out glaringly before long because it will look much more faded than the surrounding gelcoat. Soft Scrub also leaves a powdery or gritty residue, even after being hosed off. That fine layer of grit will be ground into the gelcoat as you walk on it or rub past it, slowly deteriorating the coat of wax on the gelcoat. The best product to use for stains that don't come off with soap and water is a cleaner wax, which is wax that has a rubbing compound mixed into it. The next chapter covers all you need to know about using wax to clean and protect your boat.

I would also advise against using Soft Scrub or other abrasive powder cleaners such as Ajax on vinyl fabrics and nonskid decks. Instead, I often use the Mr. Clean Magic Eraser pad (Extra Power), which you can buy at most grocery or household variety stores. But I must warn you of a few very important things before using a Magic Eraser on your boat. First, it can be very addicting. Second, it can be harmful. The Magic Eraser is like an extremely mild SOS pad or a very soft pumice stone—which is to say that it's constructed of a very fine abrasive (what Procter & Gamble calls "microbristles"), and this, rather than a chemical agent, is what makes it effective. And it does such a great job of removing marks and stains that you'll want to use it on every surface of your boat. This is why it's so addictive. The reason why it's so harmful is because using it is almost the equivalent of wet-sanding the gelcoat. It will surely remove any stain or mark you're trying to clean,

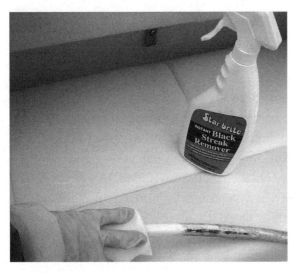

The Magic Eraser pad is ideal for cleaning power cords and other rubberized items.

but it will also remove a light layer of gelcoat and leave you with a dull section that is no longer protected by wax.

Use magic pads to clean only nonskid vinyl and rubber. Never use a Magic Eraser or other magic pad to clean a stain or a mark on smooth gelcoat unless you plan to reapply wax to that section. When nonskid starts to look gray or you see grease stains that don't come out, lightly run a wet magic pad over the nonskid. You can use a spray cleaner like Simple Green if the stain has been there for a while and doesn't come out with a first pass, but a wet magic pad should take care of most stains and marks. If your vinyl seats

are looking gray or have stains on them, spray them with Black Streak Remover, then evenly wipe them with the magic pad. Hose off the seats and they'll look new again. You can also use a magic pad to clean the shore-power cord or the rubber pontoons on your tender.

Next on the list are products that are good for cleaning windows—be they rigid portlights or deckhouse windows of glass, Lexan, or Plexiglas, or flexible boat-curtain windows of Isenglass or Strataglass. I don't recommend using a product like Windex because it can cause hazing on most of these materials. A household product that is often used on boats and does an excellent job is a window cleaner called Sprayway Glass Cleaner. It doesn't streak or cause hazing and can be used on all surfaces and materials, including Lexan, Isenglass, and wood veneers. Another good window cleaner is Mer-maids Plastic Cleaner. It is made specifically for boat windows of all materials and doesn't streak or leave a haze. I go into more detail on windows in Chapter 6—Canvas, Carpet, Vinyl, and Plastic Windows.

Sometimes it's handy to have a spray cleaner that you can use to wipe off water or bird-dropping stains between washes. The best spray cleaners I've found for this purpose are Simple Green (or Simple Green Marine), Black Streak Remover, and Krazy Clean. Avoid all-around spray cleaners like Fantastik because they cause yellowing of the gelcoat. Simple Green is less expensive at grocery or variety stores than at boat supply stores. Krazy Clean and Black Streak Remover are sold only at boat supply stores. Simple Green is the most environmentally friendly of the trio, but if you're spraying the cleaner on your boat and wiping it off (as opposed to hosing it off into the water), you can use Krazy Clean or Black Streak Remover on extra-stubborn stains. Most spray cleaners, however, should not be sprayed directly onto gelcoat because they may cause yellowing. Spray the cleaner onto a rag or a soft brush, then apply to the gelcoat, following up with a clean, dry rag to remove the cleaner. Avoid doing this type of cleaning (spray and wipe) in direct sunlight, where it may cause streaks or temporary discoloration in the gelcoat.

Rags and Squeegees

Microfiber rags are the best type to use on almost every area and finish on your boat. You can buy a large pack of them at a bulk variety store such as Costco or Sam's Club. Walmart also carries large packs for a good price. Most boat supply stores sell them, but you'll pay a lot more for a smaller pack. Microfiber rags are smooth, extremely absorbent, and long lasting, and they allow you to apply an even pressure when wiping or buffing something off. You can wash them over and over again, but do not use a fabric softener of any kind with them. They'll lose all absorbency and will cause streaking when used to wipe windows or mirrors. Terrycloth towels are not the best choice for removing cleaning products (spray cleaners or wax) because they aren't very absorbent, they wear out after several washes, and they don't provide an even pressure when wiping because of their piled surface. Older terrycloth towels can also lightly scratch fine surfaces. And you never want to use a terrycloth towel (new or old) on plastic windows.

The best squeegee I've used is the California Water Blade. You can find it at boat and auto supply stores and most household variety stores. Buy the larger rectangular blade (it usually has a purple handle) rather than the smaller blade with angled corners. One pass over the gelcoat or a window removes all water. It's easy to use correctly and won't hurt your wrist even after squeegeeing your whole boat. You will rarely have to follow up with a rag after using the Water Blade on gelcoat or windows, but if you do, use a microfiber rag. One rag is most likely all you'll need, because the squeegee will remove most of the water.

Brushes

If you want to give your boat a thorough wash (for example, cleaning all surface areas, nooks and crannies, hatch gutters, and drainage holes), you'll need four types of brushes: two deck brushes with soft and coarse brush heads that attach to a long handle, and two hand brushes with soft and coarse brush heads.

Make sure the long pole handle is made of aluminum so it's lightweight and floats. Long deck brush handles can be fairly expensive at boat supply stores, and the last thing you want is to watch yours sink straight to the bottom of the lake or harbor when you accidentally drop it overboard. You need to buy only one handle; the deck brush heads are detachable so you can swap between them. One soft and one coarse brush head will cover the majority of boat washing chores.

The soft head should be soft enough that it doesn't feel scratchy when you run it over your face. This is the brush to use on all smooth gelcoat. If you're using Shurhold products, the blue brush head is their soft brush; West Marine's soft brush is yellow. Again, if a brush is soft enough for your face, it's soft enough for smooth gelcoat.

Most deck brushes come in a medium-grade coarse and a heavy-grade coarse. There is no reason to buy both because the medium grade is coarse enough and is all you'll need. This is what you'll use on nonskid and possibly when trying to remove waterline scum that a soft deck brush won't touch. Shurhold's medium-coarse brush head is yellow. (The white one is their heavy-grade coarse.) West Marine's medium-coarse brush head is blue.

The remaining brushes you'll need are smaller hand brushes for hard-to-reach places or for use on narrow side decks or walkways where a deck brush attached to a long pole would be awkward. Here, too, you should have a soft one for

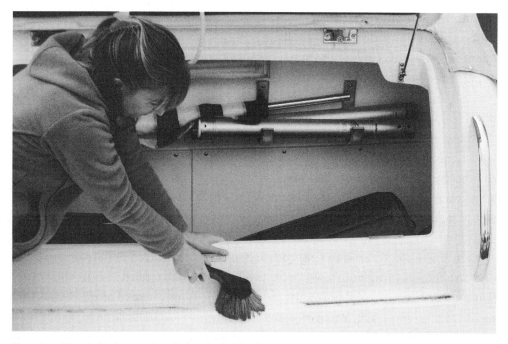

Use a hand brush in places where balancing with a heavier long-poled brush is too difficult.

smooth gelcoat and a coarse one for nonskid surfaces. You can buy these brushes in the household cleaning or auto section of most stores.

Water Filters and Softeners

If you want a spot-free boat when you're done washing it, or if you moor your boat in an area with hard water that leaves mineral deposits and other particles that produce spots, you may want to consider buying an in-line water filter and/or water softener. The culprit is not the water itself; rather it's all the minerals that exist in every drop of water. These minerals remain on paint or gelcoat long after the water has evaporated, etching permanent spots into the finish. Minerals, particularly calcium and magnesium, are what make water "hard." The calcium and magnesium actually harden into deposits called "scale" inside pipes and on other surfaces, including your boat. The only way to avoid such deposits is with a water softener. It works by replacing the calcium and magnesium ions with sodium ions, which are "soft" and don't produce scale or stains. Sodium ions make the water feel "slippery," and this causes it to sheet off surfaces more effectively; any water that remains on the boat's finish will not leave spots.

Sediment is rust or sand inside freshwater supply pipes. A broken water main miles away from your hose can allow sand to enter your water supply. Likewise, a little rust anywhere along the line can flake off into the water and pass through your hose. A sediment filter traps fine sediment as the water passes through so that nothing hits your boat but pure water. If you don't have a hard water problem, you may not need a water filter attached to your hose, although having one would reduce any sort of water spotting and make attaining a spot-free boat much easier.

In-line water filters can run from $50 to several hundred dollars. If you need one only for washing your own boat, the less expensive models will work fine. You'll simply need to add more salts or replace the filter every so often, depending on how much you use it. You can search the Internet for an "in-line hose filter" to learn more about your options, and you can purchase filters through most auto detailing stores or websites.

Other Cleaning Gear

You might think that hoses and nozzles are self-explanatory, yet there are several issues to consider. Your good ole garden hose from home isn't the best type to use around your boat, simply because garden hoses are fairly stiff and thus difficult to coil and store in a small space. I equip my crew with a typical ⅝-inch-diameter round green multipurpose hose. Make sure your hose is 20 to 30 feet longer than your boat so it will reach easily from the spigot to the far side of your deckhouse or the far corner of your flybridge. Also, be sure to clean the outside of your hose every now and then so it doesn't leave marks on your boat, especially if the hose has come in contact with a creosote piling.

Plastic nozzles are better for our purposes than heavy-duty metal ones. Not only are they cheaper, they won't leave scratch marks when inadvertently dropped on deck and won't sink if accidentally knocked overboard.

You'll need a bucket, of course. Any 3- or 5-gallon bucket will do. 'Nuff said.

Cleaning Gear and Supplies Checklist

Here is a quick checklist you can take to the store or consult to make sure you have everything you need on your boat or in your dock box:

- ▶ Bucket, multipurpose hose, and plastic nozzle
- ▶ One or two long deck brush poles
- ▶ Soft deck brush attachment and medium-coarse deck brush attachment
- ▶ Soft hand brush and coarse hand brush
- ▶ Microfiber rags and/or a squeegee
- ▶ Boat soap
- ▶ Mr. Clean Magic Eraser pads (Extra Power)
- ▶ Stain remover spray such as Simple Green, Black Streak Remover, or Krazy Clean to remove stubborn stains
- ▶ Window cleaner spray such as Sprayway Glass Cleaner or Mer-maids Plastic Cleaner to clean glass or plastic windows
- ▶ Mildew remover spray such as Tilex or Lysol

Preparation

Once you have the gear and supplies you need for washing your boat, there are a few other items you'll want to consider to make the job easier and safer.

Clothing

Make sure you're wearing comfortable clothing that will keep you warm or cool enough while you're working. Layers are best, since you'll warm up as you start working. Clothing without a lot of zippers or rivets (on jeans) is best to avoid scratching smooth gelcoat surfaces as you brush against them. Tennis shoes or deck shoes with good traction are best, but make sure the soles are non-marking or you'll be cleaning up after yourself from scuff marks everywhere you go. Polarized sunglasses cut the glare and will help you see stains or streaks that you might not otherwise notice. Except in summer, I normally wash boats wearing rubber gloves. They keep your hands warm and dry in colder weather and protect your hands from drying out after being wet for long periods of time.

Safety

As with all boating activities, washing and cleaning your boat require you to be aware of your footing and maintain your balance and coordination. When a boat is wet and sudsy, it can also be slippery, even on the nonskid. Take your time and move more slowly in wet and sudsy places. If backing up while washing an area, peek behind you to make sure you're not about to trip on a step or cleat. If leaning against a railing, make sure it's sturdy enough to hold you. And if it's been a while since you've done something that requires this much physical activity, take it slow and divide the boat into sections.

Getting Started: Step-by-Step

Before you wet your boat with the hose, look over the smooth gelcoat areas for water stains, black marks, and scuff marks. If these don't come off or lighten when you rub your finger over them, chances are a soft wash mitt and soap won't faze them either. If it's been a while since you last washed your boat, spray Simple Green over those areas (this is the one cleaner you can spray directly on your boat with no worry that it will cause yellowing or discoloration) and let it soak in while you're assembling the rest of your gear. By the time you are ready to wash those areas, the streaks or stains should come off during the first pass.

Pour a capful or two of boat soap in a bucket and fill the bucket with water, trying not to ingest the suds as the power of the hose sends them flying in your face. While you're filling the bucket, mentally divide your boat into sections so the job of washing it doesn't seem so overwhelming, especially if this is your boat's spring cleaning. The sections might include the flybridge (or helm area), port side, starboard side, bow, stern, and hull. Plan on taking a short break after each section if you need to. Always wash from the top down and from front to back. This way, the water and dirt particles will drain down and aft as you're cleaning, and you won't have to repeat any steps.

Start hosing down the boat. This will at least remove the first layer of bird droppings, dust, loose dirt in the nonskid, and leaves or other natural debris. If your boat hasn't been washed in a long time (more than three months), you may need to wash and scrub certain areas twice. If the soap isn't cutting through the dirt and the Simple Green didn't remove a stubborn stain, you can try a slightly stronger spray cleaner like Black Streak Remover or Krazy Clean. Spray the product directly onto your brush, not the boat, to prevent yellowing. Use the soft brushes on the smooth gelcoat and the medium-coarse brushes on the nonskid.

To really get your nonskid clean, hose it down and use the medium-coarse deck brush with the long handle to remove the dirt. You may have to scrub the nonskid in multiple directions or in small circles to get the brush bristles into the tiny nonskid valleys. If soap and water don't do the job, try using the Mr. Clean Magic Eraser pad with water or a spray cleaner to remove tough stains, such as grease, scuff marks, blood, and stains from bird or spider droppings.

> **Note:** You can use your soft deck or hand brush on windows to get them clean, but be sure to quickly rinse well so soap streaks don't set in, especially if you're washing in direct sunlight or on a warm day. Follow up by using a squeegee to remove drops of water and prevent water spots.
>
> Do not use any of your brushes, even the soft ones, to wash plastic windows. It doesn't take much to permanently scratch these materials, and most deck brushes aren't soft enough. Hose off the plastic windows each time you wash your boat; then wipe them clean with a microfiber cloth. Chapter 6, "Canvas, Carpet, Vinyl, and Plastic Windows," offers more detailed information on keeping plastic windows clean and scratch-free.

Don't forget to lift up the hatches and clean their tracks and gutters. If you haven't washed your boat for several months, leaves or other debris might be causing a backup in the deck drainage. If a drain is clogged, place your hose nozzle into the mouth of the drain and spray at full pressure for 30 to 60 seconds. This should push debris through the drain and unclog it.

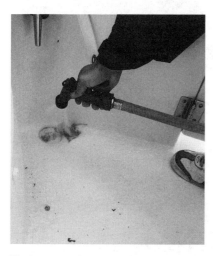

Hosing out a clogged drain

Fallen leaves and leaf parts can easily clog drains.

Once you have washed your boat's superstructure and decks, you're ready to wash the hull. If you're lucky enough to have a dock on both sides of your boat, this task will be easy. If there's a dock on only one side, however, you can still reach a good portion of the hull on the other side but most likely not all of it—unless you use a dinghy. I advise my customers to turn their boat in its berth every now and then so my crew can more thoroughly wash the other side. To reach the far side of the hull from the deck, make sure you can safely lean against your railing. Take the long-handled pole brush with the soft deck brush attachment and carefully lean over the railing to wash the hull. Don't try to reach every inch of it, because the chances of ending up in the water increase the farther you lean. The hose spray will easily reach what you can't, and hosing off the hull is better than nothing, especially if your boat has salt on it.

Once you've washed the outboard side of the hull from the deck, step down to the dock with your gear to wash the dock side. This should be easy, because you'll finally be able to stand up straight. If scum on the waterline does not come off with the soft deck brush, try using the medium-coarse brush there. If there are brown algae stains

> **Tip:** Don't leave your boat soapy for long, especially on a sunny day, or the soap will leave streak marks even after it's hosed off. If you want a streak-free finish, rinse often and thoroughly and use a squeegee, a microfiber rag, or a chamois to dry the boat after washing it.

Stubborn brown algae stains

on the hull, spray the area with Rust SprayAway, use the soft deck brush to wipe it around, then hose it off thoroughly.

Stains That Discolor Gelcoat

You may come across a few stains or marks that do not come out with soap and water or the stronger spray cleaners. These might include bird dropping residue, gray water stains (from dirty water or acid rain), yellow or purple marks left by fallen leaves, and other such stains that discolor the gelcoat. If a stain doesn't come off after three tries with my usual cleaners, I leave it for later and continue washing the rest of the boat. Removing stains like that requires a different set of products.

Bird droppings and leaves typically produce a red, yellow, or purple discoloration on your gelcoat. Things can get really messy in the fall when birds have been feasting on berries, turning your otherwise clean boat into a Picasso masterpiece. Once you've washed your boat to remove the top layer of dirt and as many of the leaves and bird droppings as will come off, head to your dock box to grab a Mr. Clean Magic Eraser pad, a bottle of cleaner wax, and a microfiber rag. I go into more detail about waxing your boat in the next chapter, but for now we need some wax to help remove these stubborn stains.

Wet a magic pad and lightly scrub the stained area to take out the discoloration. This will help remove the thin layer of gelcoat that the stain is sitting on as well as any wax in that area. Most of the stain will disappear, but not all of it. You'll be left with a much lighter stain. At this point, you can do one of two things. You can leave it for a few days while the sun bleaches it out, or you can continue to remove the stain with cleaner wax. If you choose the latter, pour a small circle of cleaner wax onto the stain and work it in with the microfiber rag until the stain comes out. It will require hard pressure to remove the stain completely. Your stain is now gone, and that area is again protected with wax. If you chose to let the sun remove the stain for you, go back a few days later; if the stain is gone, apply a coat of wax to that area to protect it again.

Removing Acid Rain, Water Spots, and Streaks

You can try washing away water stains as many times as you like, but after each rain they will sneak their way back onto your boat, black streaks dripping down each side, making it look as if you never washed it. If it's raining right now, water stains are forming as you read this! Water stains can't completely be avoided, but they can be minimized, or the path of the water run-off can be redirected. This section explains the different types of water stains, how they're made, and how to treat and prevent them.

Water spots. Water spots are caused by water from the hose, rain, or salt spray sitting on your boat's gelcoat or windows. When that drop of water evaporates, it can leave behind mineral deposits or salt crystals, making a slight outline of the drop of water on that surface. On a hot, sunny day, the sun can bake that deposit into gelcoat, glass, or plastic, causing a water spot that can no longer be washed off. This is very common if you don't squeegee your windows dry after each wash or drenching—and who can be available to do this every time it rains? Those water spots may need waxing and buffing to thoroughly remove them. Before going through the hassle of waxing those waters spots away, however, try washing your boat with white vinegar. The mineral deposits can sometimes be removed with an acidic substance, and white vinegar is the safest, cheapest, and most effective acid wash available. If that doesn't work, see Chapter 2, which discusses waxing off those stubborn water spots.

Acid rain. You may come across gray streaks on your boat's gelcoat that don't look like typical water stains (which are usually spotted grayish-black streaks) and don't come off when rubbed with your finger or washed with a soapy sponge. These streaks might be caused by acid rain. Sulfur dioxide and nitrogen oxides in the atmosphere are the primary causes of acid rain. In the United States, about two-thirds of all sulfur dioxide and one-fourth of all nitrogen oxides come from electric power generation that relies on burning fossil fuels like coal. Acid rain occurs when these gases react in the atmosphere with water, oxygen, and other chemicals to form various acidic compounds. The result is a mild solution of sulfuric acid and nitric acid in the rain. Don't bother trying to wash the stains away or wax them off. The sun will bleach them away as quickly as they were made. Trying to remove them yourself with cleaners or rubbing compound will only remove the wax in that area, and strong rubbing compound may remove a slight layer of gelcoat in the process. Best to let the sun do the job.

Water streaks. A water streak, on the other hand, is a stain caused by the dirt, minerals, and pollutants in water or rain that has penetrated into the gelcoat rather than sitting on top of it. That's why water streaks don't always wash away easily. These, as mentioned above, are the typical grayish-black streaks that often run down the sides of the flybridge and just below the rubrail. If these streaks don't come out after washing the area with soap and water, try spraying Simple Green or white vinegar to remove the stains they make. If this doesn't work, they'll need to be waxed away. I have detailed a few boats that had such bad water stains that we had to use heavy-duty rubbing com-

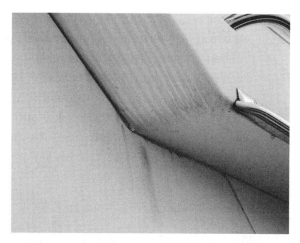

Water stains after just a few hours of rain

pound to remove them. One boat had not been waxed in several years and was not washed on a regular basis. The water stains built up over time in localized places and "soaked" into the unprotected gelcoat. Water stains are so easily preventable that there is no reason why they should ever get to that point. Keep your boat waxed and washed regularly, and nothing will soak in permanently.

One of the best ways to prevent water streaks is to redirect them so that water running down your boat drains somewhere other than onto the gelcoat. This is not possible with every water streak, but in some areas you might be able to attach a plastic tube to the end of a drainage route so the water drains off your boat rather than down an edge or the side of your boat.

Treating Mildew

In wet or humid climates, you will often find green mildew growing in rubrails, on canvas, and even on smooth gelcoat, as well as black mildew (which looks like small black specs) in the nonskid. The best way to remove mildew from your boat is with a mildew cleaner spray such as Lysol or Tilex. These products are not made specifically for boats and are far from biodegradable. In fact, the chemicals in them are so harsh that I suggest you wear rubber gloves when working with them and try not to breathe the spray particles floating in the air. If the day is at all breezy, stand so the spray is blowing away from you. I often wear a face mask if I'm working on a large area or in an enclosed flybridge. The reason I suggest using this type of cleaner, which doesn't meet any of my usual criteria for boat cleaning products, is because it works so well and makes the job a lot easier. If you can spray the product on and wipe it off with a rag, you're not hurting the environment as much as you would be if you used a brush and hosed it off. If you do have to use a brush and hose, rinse thoroughly to dilute the amount of mildew cleaner you used. A product called Mold Off (www.moldoff.org) treats and prevents mildew and is actually biodegradable (and smells good). Although I have found it to work better on canvas than on gelcoat or nonskid, it's a more environmentally safe mildew killer than Lysol Mildew Remover or Tilex Mold and Mildew Spray.

Black mold in nonskid

Once you've donned your rubber gloves and face mask, you're ready to begin. If the mold is in your nonskid, generously spray the surface with the mildew remover spray and let it soak in for a few minutes.

Then take your soft or medium-coarse deck brush and brush it around over the nonskid. You can dip the brush in a bucket of soap and water, but you don't have to. When the mildew has disappeared, hose it off thoroughly. If you find mildew on smooth gelcoat, simply pour a little mildew spray in with the soap and water and wash your boat as you normally would. If the mildew is on canvas, spray those areas with mildew remover spray, scrub the area with a soft brush, then hose it off. Mildew loves canvas, so more mildew treatment and prevention tips for canvas appear in Chapter 6.

Washing the Tender

All of the gear and supplies you use to wash your boat will work well for washing your fiberglass dinghy. If you own an inflatable, however, you might also want to purchase a product aptly named Inflatable Boat Cleaner (or something similar that is created specifically for cleaning inflatable boats or rubber materials), especially if you haven't washed your tender in a long time and there are black or gray streaks or stains on the rubber pontoons.

Assuming your tender is out of the water (as it should be for proper storage) and hanging from a davit or sitting on V-bars, make sure the drain plug is out and free of debris so all of the water you spray into the tender will easily drain out. Hose the tender down completely and let the water run off. Then spray the boat cleaner all over the rubber pontoons and any vinyl seat cushions as well. Let the spray sit on those areas for one to two minutes. It will not discolor or further stain the pontoons. Then scrub all areas of the rubber pontoons and vinyl seats with a soft or medium-coarse hand brush. This will work the product in and lift dirt, water streaks, grease marks, and other stains. Once you've run the brush over all such areas, hose them off well. This will show you just how much dirt was removed, and whether you'll need to repeat the process to remove additional dirt and stains. To remove stubborn water streaks or stains that don't come off with a first pass, try wiping or scrubbing the pontoons with a magic pad. This should remove most streaks when used along with the Inflatable Boat Cleaner spray.

Wash a fiberglass dinghy the same way you washed the smooth gelcoat sections of your boat—with a soft hand brush and soapy water. Rinse well. Then lift up seat cushions and open hatches and storage compartments and hose and scrub them clean. When finished, dry the seat cushions and instrument dash area (if any) with a towel.

Keeping Your Boat Clean on a Regular Basis

If you have no time and even less energy or enthusiasm for washing your boat after a day of cruising or sailing, at least spend five minutes hosing it down to remove salt spray, fresh bird droppings, Uncle Marvin's spilled beer now dripping into the lazarette, footprint dirt in the nonskid, and the ketchup slowly running down your brand-new Isenglass from Aunt Reba's juicy hamburger. This will prevent these stains and dirt from setting, soaking, or baking in and will make your next wash go a lot faster.

I recommend washing your boat every couple of weeks—or once a month if you keep it in a covered slip. If you wash it on a regular basis, the water stains will come off with soap and water and a swipe of your soft brush or mitt. No need to scrub harder or longer with special products. The bird droppings won't have a chance to stain your gelcoat or canvas, and dirt and debris won't get ground in to the point of scratching the fiberglass or clogging deck drains.

CHAPTER **2**

Waxing Your Boat

I'm always amazed that so many owners of fiberglass boats fail to wax their boats on a regular basis. This is the easiest, fastest, and cheapest way to protect your boat's gelcoat from harmful UV rays and other elements, keep it cleaner longer, and keep that new, glossy look. It doesn't matter if you keep your boat in a covered slip or if you've created a canvas tent to protect your baby from the elements—you still need to wax your boat!

Before we get down to it, let's begin with a quick overview of the surfaces we're protecting—fiberglass and gelcoat.

A Brief Explanation of Fiberglass Construction

Ninety-five percent of all pleasure boats manufactured during the past 40 years have hulls and decks built of fiberglass-reinforced plastic (FRP), commonly known as fiberglass. Glass fibers provide most of the strength in the FRP matrix, and a plastic resin (usually polyester but sometimes vinylester or epoxy) provides the medium within which the glass is deployed, shaped (while the resin is liquid), and ultimately immobilized (when the resin cures into a solid). Fiberglass boats are built of layers of fiberglass laid one atop the other according to a laminate schedule prescribed by the builder. In production boatbuilding, laminates are laid down from outermost to innermost layer in a female mold. The hull and deck are laminated separately, then glassed, glued, and bolted together after being removed from their respective molds.

The first step in the lamination of a hull or deck in its mold, even before the outermost layer of fiberglass is laid down, is to spray on a uniform layer of polyester gelcoat that is about 15 to 20 mils thick. (One mil equals one one-thousandth of an inch.) The gelcoat contains pigments, fillers, and additives designed to serve as a barrier to the elements (similar to the paint on a car body, which helps prevent oxidation and rust formation). Since the interior surface of the mold is mirror smooth and highly polished, the gelcoat surfaces of a new boat should in theory be shiny, smooth, and unblemished.

Most early fiberglass boats have a solid fiberglass hull and deck. A section through the hull of such a boat would show an uninterrupted lamination of fiberglass between the outer gelcoat and the inner surface. The thickness of the lamination in a 30-foot boat might range from ⅛ inch at the toe rail to ½ inch or more at the keel. A bigger boat is likely to have thicker sections.

Beginning in the 1970s, however, boatbuilders found that they could make stronger, lighter boats by using composite FRP construction, in which the hull and deck are manufactured like a sandwich. Essentially, a composite hull or deck includes three structural layers (not counting the gelcoat, which is cosmetic, not structural): (1) the outer fiberglass laminate; (2) a lightweight core, usually balsa or foam; and (3) the inner fiberglass laminate. These three layers are chemically bonded together by impregnating the sandwich with resin. A cored deck or hull can be three or four times as thick as its uncored counterpart, yet weigh no more, so it is stiffer, stronger, and more resistant to bending and flexing.

Fiberglass boats have long been advertised as being virtually maintenance-free and indestructible, but both claims are exaggerated. True, fiberglass boats are certainly much easier to maintain than wooden boats, and fiberglass boats built in the 1960s and 1970s are still going strong today. But fiberglass boats are not immune to the ravages of time and the elements.

For one thing, gelcoat is not perfectly flat. It contains microscopic cavities that resemble Swiss cheese when viewed at high magnification. The gelcoat, pockmarked with these microscopic cavities, acts like a sponge and collects water-soluble materials such as salt and dust particles.

If the boat is not waxed regularly, the gelcoat will become oxidized, which causes the FRP to appear chalky, yellow, or dull. Furthermore, the trapped water-soluble materials become wet and expand, causing pressure within the cavities and eventually forming microscopic cracks. This condition is known as gelcoat blistering. Untreated blistering can cause pockets of holes to form in the gelcoat, allowing water to seep into the underlying laminate and into the core of a composite boat. If the core is exposed to water, which acts as a solvent, it will chemically break down. This eventually leads to hull or deck failure.

On average a "healthy" FRP boat will absorb 3 percent of its weight in water, whereas an FRP boat with gelcoat blistering might absorb 10 percent or more of its weight in water. This reduces cruising performance and substantially increases fuel consumption, often by 25 percent or more. And if water wicks into the core and a structural hull or deck failure results, the boat's resale value will be adversely affected. The cost of repairing or replacing an FRP deck or hull can run 20 percent or more of the original purchase price of the boat. The cost of blister repair can run up to 10 percent or more of the boat's purchase price. Both repairs are very expensive when compared with the small cost of preventative detailing.

Granted, there are other avenues besides porous gelcoat for water to penetrate a hull or deck laminate. Deck hardware fastener holes, the hull-deck joint, and cracks, chips, and gouges in the hull or deck are common culprits. But the foregoing discussion should make clear that keeping your gelcoat sealed is an excellent idea.

That's the technical information that should send you running straight to the garage to dust off your power buffer, racing over to your nearest boat supply store to buy some wax, then gleefully skipping down to your boat to wax it. Of course, that's what you set out to do a year ago, and you have yet to finish "that project." Unfortunately, that very important task plummeted to the bottom of your Honey-Do list as soon as you bought that new "easy to assemble" gas grill last spring (which you also have yet to finish, but I can't help you with that).

Let's get down to business. You can easily wax your boat in one weekend if you're 17 years old and still have cartilage in your knees and elbows. But if you're somewhat older than that, you'll need a good plan of attack to substitute for youthful exuberance, flexibility, and stamina. I break this task down for you so it no longer seems insurmountable and can be done in one week or over a couple of weekends. The more oxidized your boat is, the more work it will take, but if you tackle your boat in sections, the job won't seem so overwhelming. If your boat is new or has only light oxidation, it won't take as long to wax and you'll have plenty of extra time to assemble that gas grill, with no more excuses.

This chapter covers:

- ▶ Waxing your boat
- ▶ Preparation and safety
- ▶ Gear and supplies
- ▶ Waxing step-by-step
- ▶ Maintaining an Awlgrip topcoat

About Waxing Your Boat

How Often

It's fairly easy to figure out when you need to wax your boat because the gelcoat will tell you by appearing faded rather than shiny. Water fails to bead up or dissipate as it does after a fresh coat of wax is applied, and water sits longer on wax-starved gelcoat without evaporating. You'll want to wax your boat before it shows you how thirsty it is for wax, however; otherwise, there will be a period of time during which the sun and other elements will slowly cause the wax-starved gelcoat to deteriorate.

To repeat, there are two reasons to wax your boat. The first is to protect the gelcoat, and since I'm a die-hard practical person, that's always my first concern. But if you have a newer boat or use enough rubbing compound on an older boat, you'll be able to get it glossy again, too. This is the added benefit of a good wax job. Wax your boat to protect it, and the gloss will show itself to you.

Waxing your boat on a regular basis will help maintain and possibly improve its resale value. A clean boat shows prospective buyers that it is well cared for, and this silent message attracts buyers even in a difficult market. Brokers will be happy to take your listing, since your boat will show well.

There is no standard rule for how often you should wax your boat. A boat that is kept in a covered slip and spends little or no time in salt water or direct sunlight could easily get by being waxed every 12 months. At the other extreme, a boat that is moored in salt water in a sunny climate (for example, Southern California or Florida) and is not in a covered slip should have its topside waxed every three to six months and its hull waxed every six to nine months. Between these extremes, a boat moored in an open slip in salt or fresh water but in less intense sunlight (for example, the Pacific Northwest) should have its hull and topside waxed every spring, and its topside waxed again near the end of the boating season.

The accompanying chart will help you see the big picture.

Moorage	Frequency
Not covered, full sun, and in salt water	Wax decks every 3 to 6 months; wax hull every 6 to 9 months
Not covered, mostly cloudy, and in salt or fresh water	Wax whole boat every spring; wax decks again in late summer or fall
Covered slip in salt or fresh water	Wax whole boat every 12 months.

Of course, even if you keep your boat in a covered slip, if you use it a lot during the summer where it is in direct sunlight most of the time or constantly getting hit with salt spray, you may want to decrease the time between wax jobs, at least for the topsides. And rinsing your boat with fresh water on a regular basis will help prevent salt from etching water spots into the gelcoat.

Determine Your Gelcoat's Condition

The accompanying chart describes five gelcoat conditions based on degrees of oxidation. This will help you determine which wax products, compounds, and equipment to use as we get further into the chapter.

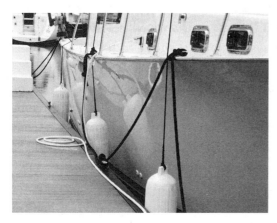

A glossy hull just after being waxed

An oxidized hull

Level	Gelcoat Condition	Description
1	Glossy (no oxidation)	"Like-new" gloss, typical of a boat that is less than a year old and is kept in a covered slip or in a non-sunny climate.
2	Sheen (light oxidation)	The gloss is starting to fade in places, usually on the topside first (especially the brow), but there is still a slight gloss or sheen on the gelcoat.
3	Faded (medium oxidation)	The gelcoat appears to have a matte finish with no gloss left, but when you run your finger over it, there's no chalkiness. The hull may still have a sheen, but the topside is mostly matte.
4	Chalky (heavy oxidation)	There's no gloss left, and your finger picks up a chalky residue when run over the gelcoat. On a colored surface—say a blue hull—you'll see a white haze fading the color out.
5	Chalky and pitted	The boat is so oxidized (usually an older boat that's rarely been waxed) that even a heavy-duty rubbing compound doesn't make much of a difference. The gelcoat may be thin, and because it hasn't been protected with wax, it may be riddled with small pinholes or pits. In this case the gelcoat might need to be lightly wet sanded to cut through the oxidized layer and give you a new base to work with.

The topside and the hull can be at different levels of oxidation because the topside is exposed to more direct sunlight and weather. It's common for the hull to be a level 1 or 2 while the topside is a level 2 or 3.

Two additional factors will affect the way you work with your gelcoat and what results you can expect from it. Those factors are the gelcoat's thickness and its quality (including the quality of its application). Every manufacturer uses a different type and quality of gelcoat, and there is more than one way to apply it (for example, rolled on or sprayed on). As a detailer who has worked on many different production boats, I have learned which manufacturers use high-quality gelcoat because it makes our job of waxing boats much easier. We know that no matter how long the owner has let the boat go, high-quality gelcoat will easily come back to a glossy state.

Lower-quality or thinly applied gelcoat will be more difficult to bring back to a glossy state and will require more rubbing compound. You know you're looking at thin gelcoat when you can actually see the fiberglass weave pattern through the gelcoat. (This is called "print-through.") You will rarely be able to achieve a glossy finish on any section exhibiting print-through because there are too many surface deviations for the light to reflect perfectly.

Some manufacturers use quality gelcoat, yet for whatever reason (maybe having to do with how the gelcoat was applied), wax swirls easily, and it is almost impossible to keep swirls out of the finish even if you use a soft wax with no compound in it, applying and removing it by hand. You will be able to see those swirls only when the boat is sitting in direct sunlight. By the way, this is the only benefit of waxing a boat in direct sunlight—to make sure you're not making any swirls as you go. If you find that you are, you can make a mid-course correction in the wax products you're using or in your technique of applying and removing the wax.

It's easier to check for swirl marks in direct sunlight.

One-Step or Multistep Procedures (or What's It Going to Take?)

Once you have a better understanding of your gelcoat's present condition, you'll have a better idea of just what it's going to take to bring it back to glossy. I consider "glossy" the ultimate, aspirational goal, because if the boat looks glossy, it means there is no oxidation on the gelcoat. There are typically three approaches you can take to bring a boat back to glossy, and which of the three you use will depend on the gelcoat's condition and on how long you hope the wax job to last.

▶ The one-step approach uses either a soft wax (with no rubbing compound in it) or a cleaner wax (a mixture of compound and wax) to protect the gelcoat and bring it back to glossy. On brand-new boats or on boats with light to medium oxidation (level 1, 2, or 3 in the accompanying table), this is all you need to do.

▶ In a two-step approach, you do a first pass with just rubbing compound to cut through the top layer of gelcoat and remove oxidation, then a second pass with just wax to protect the gelcoat from oxidizing further. This is the approach you might choose for a boat with medium to heavy oxidation (level 3 or 4).

▶ If your boat falls into the category of level 3 or 4, and if you want to achieve that showroom gloss again or you want or need the wax job to last an extra-long time, you may choose to follow a three-step process. You would first go over the boat with compound to remove oxidation, then you would repeat with polish to seal the gelcoat, and finally you would apply and buff a coat of wax to further protect it. If you're hiring a detailer to wax your boat, expect to pay almost two or three times as much for a two- or three-step process because the detailer will go over every inch of waxable gelcoat two or three times.

A coat of wax starts to thin within three to six months after application. Some waxes claim to last 12 months or longer, to which I say sure, if you keep your boat in a boathouse and take it out only after the sun has gone down.

Preparation

It is best to start with a clean surface—one that is free of dirt and mildew. The present condition of the gelcoat—glossy or faded, chalky or pitted, swirled or swirl-free, with or without print-through—should be clearly visible so you know exactly what you're working with.

If your boat already has swirls in the gelcoat that refuse to go away while you're waxing, you'll at least know that you weren't the one who put them there. If you notice that the deck surfaces are considerably more faded than the hull, you may decide to do a two-step job on the deck structures (or maybe just the brow) and only a one-step job on the hull. If you can see the underlying fiberglass pattern through the gelcoat, you'll know that no matter how good your wax job is, it may not look perfectly glossy in that area because of the surface deviations. And so on.

Start by washing your boat and removing all dirt and mildew. Don't

> **Note:** A professional boat detailer may not fully wash your boat before waxing it *if* the boat is only a bit dusty *and* the detailer's crew knows that they'll be using a cleaner wax (wax mixed with compound) and a power buffer. A little dust is of little concern given that the rubbing compound will grind into your gelcoat to remove the top layer of oxidation. The crew should, however, fully wash the boat after waxing it to remove wax dust from all surfaces.

bother trying to remove water stains, scuff marks, or bird-dropping residues that won't come off with soap and water because the wax will remove them. Once you wash your boat, you're almost ready to start, but first let's go over a few quick pointers.

Weather and Waxing

What the weather is doing can greatly affect your wax job and even determine how you will apply the wax and how long you'll let it sit on the gelcoat before you buff it in and off. The only weather you cannot wax in is rain; wax isn't too difficult to apply in rain, but it's next to impossible to remove. You should work in rainy conditions only if you're working under a tarp or if you're working on a hull that is at such an angle that the rain isn't hitting it directly. If you're using a rubbing compound with a buffer, you can work in mist or light rain because in most cases you will buff the rubbing compound off before it dries completely. Other external conditions you should consider include:

▶ **Direct sunlight.** You'll easily be able to see if you're creating swirl marks, but the sun will cause the wax to dry faster, and if you have oxidized gelcoat (level 2 or higher) or thin, older gelcoat, the wax won't come off easily (or at all) if left to sit too long in the sun. It's best to do the job in 3-foot-square areas, applying and buffing a section at a time.

▶ **Hot day.** Even if you're waxing in the shade, you may need to work in smaller sections so the wax doesn't dry out before you can buff it. This isn't a problem with newer, still-glossy gelcoat (level 1). In fact, you could apply wax to the entire boat and then buff it off and it would still be easy to work with. If your boat's gelcoat condition is level 2 or greater, however, smaller sections are the rule in hot weather.

▶ **Temperate shade.** These are the best conditions for waxing. Although you won't easily be able to see swirl marks, you can work in larger sections because the wax won't dry fast without direct sun or excessive heat. Just remember, the porosity of the gelcoat (a function of oxidation and thickness) is even more important than sun and heat in causing wax to become hard to remove. If your gelcoat condition is level 2 or higher, always work in smaller sections so you don't have to worry about the wax drying into the gelcoat.

▶ **Rain or moisture.** It is impossible to get good results in rain, fog, or heavy humidity. You may be able to apply the wax fairly easily, but the wax has to be dry in order to be wiped or buffed off without creating splotchy results.

▶ **Cold weather.** In temperatures below, say, 40 degrees Fahrenheit, the wax either won't dry at all or will take too long to dry to a haze, leaving you standing around in the cold, waiting. It's better to wax a boat in temperatures of 45 degrees or higher (if you must do it at all in colder weather) and preferably when the sun is on the boat to help warm the gelcoat.

> *Tip:* If your boat is normally in direct sunlight on one side but shady on the other, work on the shady side, then turn the boat to work on the other side.

Waxing at a Boatyard

If your boat will be pulled out to have work done at a service yard, you may want to think twice about having it waxed in the yard. Although it can be easier to wax when the boat is out of the water, at any given time when conditions are appropriate for waxing, there is likely to be a boat getting painted somewhere in the yard, and any airborne overspray can land on your boat, causing it to turn gray in those areas as if afflicted with small gray water spots. This condition is known as the "boatyard blues." You can't feel the overspray on the gelcoat, but you can see it. Having it land on your boat is one thing, but having it get mixed in with the wax and then get buffed into your boat is another matter entirely. In the latter instance it will remain on your boat much longer, because the UV protectants in the wax will prevent the sun from being able to bleach out the overspray flecks. You will basically have waxed it into the gelcoat.

If your boat does have paint overspray on it, the best way to remove it is to apply rubbing compound or acetone to that area, which will remove the wax and top layer of overspray. (Use acetone over a smaller area, or use rubbing compound if the overspray covers a large area. Acetone is not recommended for large sections of gelcoat; nor is it human-friendly. Wear gloves and a respirator when working with acetone.) You will still be able to see gray spots, but they will be lighter than when you started. Now let the boat sit for a couple of days while the sun bleaches out the remaining stains. If your boat is in direct sunlight, this may only take 24 hours. After a few days at most, the overspray stains should be gone and you can

It's hard to avoid getting overspray, known as the "boatyard blues," on your boat at the service yard.

then re-wax that area to protect it again. If you don't want to trust the sun, or you need to remove the overspray stains immediately, simply rub much harder and for a longer period of time with rubbing compound until the stains are gone. You'll need to re-wax that area to protect it again when you're finished.

Safety and Hard-to-Reach Areas

There is no argument here—waxing a boat is hard work. It requires physical strength, agility, coordination, and balance as well as repetitive motions with your arm or wrist. Nevertheless, most anyone can do it as long as you take the necessary precautions and take your time, allowing short breaks to give yourself and your body a rest. When I started my boat detailing company at the age of 19, I could easily wash seven boats a day or wax a ski boat in four hours and do something active with my friends in the afternoon. Now, in my late thirties, I'm lucky to get three boats washed in a day without suffering an achy lower back and sore wrists and taking Advil with dinner. But don't let that scare you. The achy lower back is most likely from trying to carry all my gear to each boat rather than using a dock cart, and the sore wrists are from an unforgettable run-in with a tractor while riding a certain horse whose name I won't mention at the moment. But I digress. Take your time and divide the boat into sections so it's not so overwhelming.

On a flybridge powerboat, the brow over the windshield is probably the most difficult area to reach, especially if it's more vertical than horizontal. You'll be able to reach the lower half of the brow by standing (carefully) on the lower edge of the windshield, but be careful not to put any weight on the windshield glass or too much weight on the frames lest it weaken the seal and cause water to seep in the next time it rains or you wash your boat. You may be able to reach the top edge of the brow by leaning over the windscreen from the flybridge, but how do you reach the entire middle section? A ladder doesn't work well because it's difficult to stabilize, and even if you can make it stable enough to climb on, it won't provide a good platform from which to reach that section, especially if you're holding a buffer.

The best solution is to rappel down from the flybridge or attach a suction cup handle to the brow to use as a foothold. If you choose to rappel down, you will need a rope that is strong enough to secure you; one end of it will be tied around your waist, and the other end will be securely tied around a metal post (preferably the post of the captain's chair) in the flybridge. Once you've tied both ends and posi-

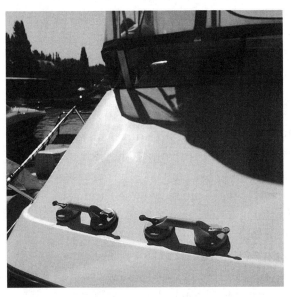

Use suction-cup handles when waxing the brow to give you something to hold onto.

tioned your gear (wax, buffer, and rags) nearby, climb out of the flybridge and over the windscreen, and slowly lower yourself, making sure you feel secure before you actually start working on this area. If the rope will be draped over the windscreen, be careful not to put your full weight on the rope if you can help it to avoid cracking or scraping the windscreen. You can then begin waxing and buffing this area safely.

The best way to reach the side of the hull away from the dock is to turn your boat. My crew and I have tried waxing boats from floating rafts and tenders, but it is more work than it's worth. For one thing, if you're using an electric buffer, there are now more opportunities for the cord to go into the water, causing an electric shock. Also, because you'll need one hand to help keep yourself in one place while working, you are left with only one hand to work the buffer, which won't allow you to get good leverage on your work and will result in a splotchy job. Even if you're waxing by hand, you may not be able to apply enough even pressure to the rag to get a smooth, even result. And if your slip has a high dock from which you can't easily reach the lower portions of the hull, you'll want to move your boat to a low dock while you complete the job.

It's much easier to reach the hull on a dock that is level with the water line.

The most important safety issue when waxing your boat is not letting the electric cord of a power buffer come in contact with water. And it can happen easily if you're not careful. The best way to prevent this accident is by wrapping the extension cord around each cleat between the power source (either the power pole at the dock or an outlet on your boat) and where you're working. Also tie the extension cord and the buffer's cord in a loose knot before plugging them into each other. This way, when you tug on the cord as you move farther down the boat, the cords won't come unplugged from each other and fall into the water. When you're working directly over water, wrap the cord nearest the buffer around your hand or forearm

Another safety concern is keeping the buffer's cord from wrapping around your neck while you're running the buffer. I know this sounds crazy, but it can happen if you're not paying attention.

This safety technique keeps the cords from coming apart while you're running the buffer.

Given just the slightest contact, the spinning head will "grab" the cord and start wrapping it around the neck of the buffer. If part of that cord is hanging over the back of your neck or shoulders (where you draped it to keep it out of your way), you can be sure your neck will become involved in the action. It will happen so fast that your face may be less than an inch from the spinning buffer pad before you realize that all you have to do to stop this impending doom is take your finger off the trigger.

To my knowledge, at the time of this writing, there has never been a reported injury or accident from someone picking up a phone and dialing the number of a boat detailer. If nothing else, you'll always have this to fall back on if for some reason you decide not to do the work yourself.

Gear and Supplies

The more oxidized your gelcoat is, the more gear you will need. A glossy boat requires less gear. It's that simple. Here's a list of all the gear and supplies you'll need to wax a boat in any condition; from this master list, based on the condition of your gelcoat, you can create your own list.

Keep in mind that waxes improve every year, and the products I list today may be outdated in a few years, or there will be new and better products on the market to replace them. In addition to naming a few brands, I include a description of what type of wax to look for in case the brands I name aren't sold in your area.

Waxing, Rubbing Compound, and Polish

Here's a scenario we're all familiar with. You've finally decided to wax your boat, so you head over to your nearest boating supply store to buy some wax. An hour later, after standing in front of all those products on the shelf that cry out "easy to use," "no rubbing—just wipe on and off," "practically waxes your boat for you," and "leaves a glossy finish for at least seven years," you are thoroughly confused, frustrated, and ready to throw in the towel. Don't give up just yet. There are many types of waxes out there, and some work better than others on certain types and conditions of gelcoat. With the following tips and advice, you'll be able to walk into the store, grab the wax you need like a pro, and go!

Many factors affect what products you should use and how you should apply and buff off the wax. Every boat manufacturer uses a slightly different gelcoat. Your boat may be faded on deck but still glossy on the hull. You may have color stripes or a colored hull that is more faded than the rest of the boat. Your boat may have slight scratches or swirl marks that are difficult to remove. Therefore, you can't always buy just one bottle of wax that will give you great results on all areas of your boat, even if your boat is brand new. You may need to buy two or three different types of wax or rubbing compound for differently oxidized sections, or you may find that mixing different waxes and rubbing compounds creates the perfect product for your gelcoat. The following list describes the different types of waxes, compounds, and polishes you'll find at your local boating store.

▶ **Carnauba or pure wax.** I also refer to this as *soft wax*, meaning that it contains no rubbing compound. It comes in liquid form in a squeeze bottle or in paste form in a metal tin. Since it contains no compound, it is best for a brand-new boat that has no oxidation (level 1) or for the finishing step in a two- or three-step process. It can easily be applied by hand or with a buffer.

> **Note:** When using a soft or pure wax (one with no buffing compound), you can use either a liquid wax from a squeeze bottle or a paste wax from a can. The results will be the same. If you're using a cleaner wax, however, liquid wax from a squeeze bottle is easier to apply properly and gives you a more even distribution of rubbing compound than paste wax from a can.

▶ **Cleaner wax.** This is a combination of wax and rubbing compound. It's the equivalent of doing a two-step wax job in one easy step. It is ideal to use on boats that have light to medium oxidation (described as level 2 or 3 in the oxidation table earlier in this chapter). There are many brands of cleaner wax on the market. Thicker, more clay-like compositions are good for medium (level 3) oxidation, whereas thinner waxes are better for lighter (level 2) oxidation. Shake the bottle, and if the contents easily move around, it's a good cleaner wax for light oxidation. If the contents don't shake much, you've found a good cleaner wax for medium oxidation.

While you're standing in front of the wax section, grab a jug of Meguiar's Cleaner Wax and shake it. Then grab a jug of 3M Cleaner Wax and shake that. You'll instantly be able to tell the difference and will have gained a better understanding of a cleaner wax meant for light oxidation (Meguiar's) and one meant for medium oxidation (3M). Although it's best to use a power buffer with any cleaner wax, a thinner formulation can be applied and buffed off by hand with fair results. This is not possible with a thicker formulation.

▶ **Restorer wax.** This type of wax is very thick, more rubbing compound than wax, and is meant for boats with heavy oxidation (level 4). If you don't have much experience working with compounds and power buffers, this type of wax is not your best choice. It's like working with pure clay. A better option is to mix other types of rubbing compounds and waxes until you find a mixture that gives you the desired result. I discuss this technique later in the chapter.

▶ **Rubbing compounds.** There are many types of compounds. To make your options less confusing, I take the extremely simplified route of categorizing them by color—either brown or white. (You may not be able to tell if a compound is brown or white unless you open the lid.) The brown compounds are thicker and are used primarily to remove heavier oxidation. Their main ingredient is clay (Tripoli). An example of this type is 3M Super Duty Rubbing Compound. The white compounds are thinner and are most often used to remove scratches, swirl marks, and light to medium oxidation, or as a finishing polish. Their main ingredient is aluminum oxide. Examples include 3M Imperial Compound and Finishing Material and 3M Finesse It Finishing Material. Remember that pure rubbing compound contains no wax, whereas cleaner wax is a mixture of rubbing compound and wax.

▶ **Polishes.** A polish doesn't have wax in it but contains other synthetic ingredients that do the job of wax. An example is Starbrite Premium Marine Polish with PTEF. PTEF is Starbrite's registered trademark name for polytetraflouroethylene, the generic version of Teflon. We're familiar with Teflon because it's on pots and pans and creates an easy-to-work-with, nonstick surface. Likewise, by polishing your boat with a similar ingredient, you're creating a smooth surface on the gelcoat that helps prevent salt spray, bird droppings, and other particles from sticking into it. It is UV resistant and can last a long time. Polishes are used on new gelcoat or gelcoat that has already had the oxidation cut through or buffed out.

Note: I refer to the 3M and Meguiar's brands simply because I use them most often and am most familiar with them. There are many other excellent brands, including Collinite, SeaPower, Interlux, and Starbrite, to name just a few. Additionally, there are specialized brands from smaller companies that you can order only online. The main thing to look for is a wax that is meant for gelcoat, provides UV protection, and either does or does not contain compound, depending on the level of oxidation in the surface you will be treating.

Applying polish by hand or with a buffer will give equally good results. Applying polish is the second step in a three-step wax process.

▶ **Copolymer sealants.** Examples of these products include the Vertglas and Poliglow systems. With these systems, you are not waxing your boat but rather sealing the gelcoat, which helps protect it from becoming more oxidized. It's like putting a hard candy shell on your gelcoat. I do not use these products on boats and do not have any experience with them, so I don't go into detail about how they work. I have heard mixed reviews about products like these, which require you to apply five or more coats in order to get the most gloss and protection for your gelcoat. Additionally, you can't apply wax over these sealants in the future if you desire but must first remove the sealant completely from the gelcoat, which requires a lot of rubbing compound.

Power Buffers

If you plan to wax your boat yourself, you should buy a power buffer. If you plan to hire a professional, however, and simply want to keep up selected areas on your own between the detailer's wax jobs, you don't need to spend $200 or so on a good polisher/buffer. The detailer will cut through the oxidation, so you can simply apply a soft wax or cleaner wax by hand to maintain the polish on the areas you're targeting.

The best power buffer I've used is the German-made Porter-Cable 9428. We wax boats five days a week year-round, running a buffer several hours a day, stopping it and starting it, getting wax dust in it and occasionally dropping it in the water, which is never good for the buffer or the unlucky person still holding the electric cord. Our Porter-Cables ran four years straight before finally dying on us. I took them in for servicing, and now they're up and running again. Unfortunately, Porter-Cable discontinued this model, so now you can buy it only on eBay or Craigs list. If you're looking for power buffers online, search for the words "variable-speed polisher," which is how these types of buffers are usually categorized.

One runner-up is the Makita 9227. This power buffer has features similar to those of the Porter-Cable 9428 and looks almost exactly the same. I purchased a few of these to replace our old Porter-Cables, and so far we've been fairly happy with them. This model is lighter than the Porter-Cable and has less vibration, but it heats up quickly. That won't affect the results, though.

Another runner-up is the DeWalt 849, but this buffer's slow-start feature is very sensitive and doesn't take much pressure on the trigger to go from slow to fast. Instead you have to be ready to start at a high speed. The body is slightly longer and heavier than the others. It also comes with a straight rather than D-shaped handle, which makes it somewhat more difficult to hold and maneuver, and it runs at a faster speed and with more torque than the others, so you have to know what you're doing before you touch it to gelcoat. All in all, it's a good buffer for an experienced operator who is strong enough to control it and is using compound on a heavily oxidized boat. The more oxidation you need to cut through, the more power you need from a buffer.

You might be able to save a few dollars if you buy a used or refurbished buffer from a reliable seller. If you'll be using it only once or twice a year, a used model in good working condition should be fine.

The buffers I've described are all variable-speed polishers/buffers and can only be purchased at large hardware stores or online. The types of buffers sold at your local boating supply store are not very effective on anything but a brand new boat that requires only a light coat of pure liquid wax with no rubbing compound in it. They are random orbital buffers and are difficult to hold properly for long periods of time. They also don't allow you to apply even pressure while you work, and you will often end up with splotchy results.

For those of you who own smaller boats (less then 25 feet in length) or ski boats, you might consider a few of the polishers/buffers that are sold for auto detailing. They have a smaller pad base (usually receiving a 5- or 6-inch buffing pad rather than a 9-inch pad), can get into tight areas, and are lighter and easier to hold. Some of these buffers include the Porter and Cable 7424 Detailing Machine, the Meguiars G-110 Dual Action Polisher and the Flex XC3401VRG Dual-Action Polisher. You can search for these online as well as for the various pads and accessories for them. One good website to start with is www.ProperAutoCare.com.

If you're going to use a power buffer, you'll also need an extension cord, a spur (a tool used to clean wax off the buffer wheel), and a power adapter (if you want to plug it into the dock rather than your boat). You will also need buffing pads for applying and buffing off wax and rubbing compound. There are wool, foam, and synthetic pads to choose from; however, I rarely get good results from the synthetic pads, so I will mostly focus on the wool and foam pads. Wool pads are best for level 2 or greater gelcoat, and foam pads are best for brand new or level 1 gelcoat. You can use a single-sided pad that attaches to the disc head with a Velcro backing plate or a double-sided pad that attaches to the disc head with a small adapter piece. A double-sided head can get into tighter spots because you can use the edges more effectively, and it's just as quick and easy to flip over for the cleaner side as it is to rip off a Velcro-backed pad and slap on a new one.

- ▶ **Wool compounding pads** are typically white (like the 3M Perfect-It III Compounding Pad or the 3M Superbuff III Buffing Pad) and are used for applying or buffing out rubbing compound on an oxidized boat (level 2 or greater).

- ▶ **Wool finishing pads** are usually yellow (like the 3M Superbuff Polishing Pad) and are used for applying or buffing off liquid wax on a new boat or cleaner wax on a level 1 or 2 boat after you've used the compounding pad with rubbing compound to remove oxidation.

- ▶ **Heavy-cut foam pads** are best for removing deeper scratches or heavy oxidation.

- ▶ **Medium-cut foam pads** have 90 percent of the cutting power of the heavy-cut pad but finishes like a polishing pad with minimum haze. Always try this pad first before using the heavy-cut pad to remove deeper swirls and scratches.

- ▶ **Mild-cut foam pads** are used for polishing to restore gloss and remove light oxidation and fine swirls.

- ▶ **No-cut foam pads** are superfine finishing pads for applying the final liquid wax or polish. This is also the pad to use for layering one wax on top of another to build up coats for added protection and shine.

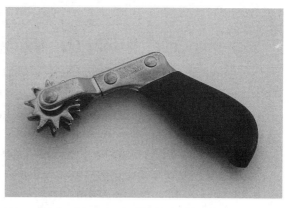

Use a spur to clean your buffing pads so they last longer.

Other Gear

The only other gear you'll need is:

▶ **Rags.** If you'll be waxing and buffing by hand, use terry cloth rags or old T-shirts to apply the wax and microfiber rags to remove it. If you're using a power buffer to buff off the wax, you'll still need a few microfiber rags to remove any remaining light haze or wax dust that the buffer doesn't get.

▶ **Squeeze bottles.** The thicker the wax, the harder it is to squeeze from the bottle it comes in. Transfer the wax to a few spare squeeze bottles (with the help of a small funnel), and use those while you're working on your boat.

▶ **Dust mask.** When you remove wax by hand or with a buffer, a fine mist of wax dust will cover everything, including you. Because the particles are so fine, you'll breathe them in if you don't wear a dust mask. I suggest wearing one if you have respiratory problems or if you're sensitive to dust and particles in the air.

Waxing Step-by-Step

In most maintenance work, 90 percent is preparation and 10 percent is the actual task. For waxing a boat, however, I would change that ratio to 30/70. Preparation is important, but technique is king. In this section I help you learn how to wax your boat based on its level of oxidation—the main deciding factor in what products and techniques you'll use.

For a Level 1 Boat (No Oxidation)

A boat attains level 1 status because it is less than a year old or because you removed all oxidation with the last wax job and have since kept the boat in a covered slip and operated it only in the shade. In other words, a pure level 1 boat is rare. On the other hand, it is not unusual for a boat to show light oxidation on areas like a brow or foredeck but retain a good gloss elsewhere. In such a case, treat the oxidized areas as level 2 and everything else as level 1.

Level 1 areas need only a soft wax, with no rubbing compound in it, or a polish. You don't want to use compound where there is no oxidation to cut through, or you'll create swirl marks or even very light scratches. You can apply the wax and buff it off either by hand or with a power buffer. If applying by hand, make sure you hold the rag or pad as flat as you can. Place your hand flat over the rag (which you've folded in half once and then in half again) to apply pressure when spreading the wax. Do not hold the rag as you would a sponge and apply pressure with your fingertips. If you apply pressure mostly with your fingertips (unless in a small area—for example, around a stanchion, where only your fingertips can fit), the wax won't be applied evenly and smoothly, and when you wipe or buff it off, the results will look splotchy. Keep your hand flat over the folded rag and apply pressure as evenly as you can in a circular motion. Go over the section you're doing a few times to make sure you cover it evenly and entirely.

You can apply the wax by hand and buff it off with a power buffer, or you can apply and buff the wax with a buffer. The same observations apply. Keep the buffer pad as flat as you can instead of tipping it or using the edges, and try to maintain an even pressure as you proceed. Uneven pressure causes the edges to bear on the gelcoat, and the result is swirl marks or splotchiness.

Soft waxes and polishes that don't contain rubbing compound can be allowed to dry to a haze before you wipe or buff them off. If you're working in the shade, you can literally wax an entire side of your boat, letting it dry to a haze, then go back and wipe or buff

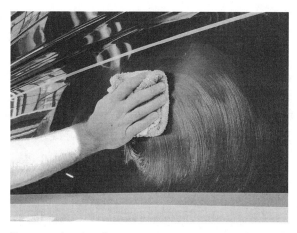

Keep your hand as flat as you can to apply even pressure.

Note: Once you've wiped the wax and wax dust from the area you were working on, view that area from several angles. If it's a sunny day, polarized sunglasses will help you see imperfections. If you see swirl marks, uneven light reflections, splotchiness, or dull spots, you should go over the area again using flat, even pressure. Try working small sections at a time. If one side of your boat is in the shade, do that side first.

Look down the side of the boat at an angle to check for splotchiness and make sure nothing was missed.

it off. In direct sunlight, however, it's better to do smaller sections at a time so the wax doesn't dry into the gelcoat and become difficult to remove.

For a Level 2 Boat (Light Oxidation)

If your boat is lightly oxidized, use a thin cleaner wax such as Meguiar's Cleaner Wax or SeaPower. You can work by hand or with a buffer, but either way be sure to use even pressure when you apply the wax. In fact, light oxidation over still-existing gloss is a condition that invites more swirl marks than any other. You want to cut through the light layer of oxidation but not scratch or swirl the still-glossy finish. A good product for this gelcoat condition is Meguiar's Flagship Premium Marine Wax. Alternatively, you can try mixing one part 3M Finesse It with two or three parts soft liquid wax.

Keep the buffer flat against the gelcoat to prevent burning and swirl marks.

Once you've applied the wax, let it dry to a haze and then wipe or buff it off. If you're using a buffer, keep the buffing pad as flat as you can against the surface of the boat to prevent swirl marks. When finished, go over the area once more with a microfiber rag to remove all wax dust and haze.

When applying wax, use a slower buffer speed for a more even application. If you're using a squeeze bottle, apply a thin line of wax directly onto the gelcoat surface and then use the buffer at a slow speed to spread or apply the wax in that section. Double the speed when it's time to buff the wax off and then follow up with a microfiber rag to remove all wax dust. For example, if your buffer offers speed levels from one to six, use level two or three to spread the wax on and level four or five to buff it in and off.

Tip: Most bottles of wax state in their instructions that you should let the wax dry to a haze before you wipe or buff it off, and this is indeed the way to proceed with thin cleaner wax on a lightly oxidized boat. If you're using thick cleaner wax or rubbing compound on a moderately (level 3) to heavily (level 4) oxidized gelcoat surface, however, it's better to buff the wax or compound off while it is still a little wet. The remaining moisture, together with the power of the buffer, will help the wax or compound cut through the oxidation.

For a Level 3 Boat (Medium Oxidation)

When your boat shows medium oxidation in most areas, a power buffer is almost a necessity. You can try to apply and remove the cleaner wax by hand, but it will be more difficult to work (read "sore wrists") and it won't cut through the oxidation as well or as evenly as you'll need to get a glossy result. It will almost definitely look splotchy when you're finished. If you don't own a power buffer and don't want to spend $200 to buy one, consider renting one from a tool rental company. If their rental fee is around $40 per day, however, and you think it might take you three or more days to wax your boat, you might as well buy a buffer. If you'll be using it only a few times a year, it will last forever. (And you can use it on your automobiles with a foam pad at slower speeds.)

To effectively remove medium oxidation, you'll want to use a thick cleaner wax such as 3M Cleaner Wax. Apply the wax by hand or with a buffer, using the buffer with a compounding pad to work it into the gelcoat while the wax is still slightly wet and then buffing it off with a finishing pad. Follow up with a micro-fiber rag to remove the wax dust. Work in small sections, and work mostly on the shaded side of the boat or at least not in direct sunlight and not on a day that is warmer than 90 degrees.

This heavily oxidized sailboat definitely needs a two-step approach.

If one type of wax that is meant for medium oxidation doesn't work as well as you were hoping, you can get creative and try mixing different waxes and compounds together. It is also at this stage that your boat may need a two-step approach—a first pass with rubbing compound and a second pass with wax—in order to remove the oxidation and bring back a glossy finish. My crew often comes across medium to heavily oxidized boats that don't respond at all to just one type of wax or compound straight from the bottle. We end up trying various mixes of wax and compounds until we find one that works on that particular quality and thickness of gelcoat and its level of oxidation. We have yet to find the one perfect mixture that works on all types of gelcoat with all levels of oxidation, and leaves a perfect finish every time. It would cost a lot of money to buy several different types of waxes and compounds, so your best bet for level 3 gelcoat is to buy one bottle of a thick cleaner wax (such as 3M Cleaner Wax), one bottle of thin rubbing compound (such as 3M Imperial Compound), and one bottle of soft wax (with no compound in it). We often mix two or more of these products until we find a combination that works well.

For a Level 4 Boat (Heavy Oxidation)

Heavy oxidation requires a two-step process. You must first remove the oxidation before you can apply wax or polish to the boat. A cleaner wax won't be strong enough to remove the oxidation; you'll need to use compound first. Once again, a mixture of a few different rubbing compounds might work best. Start with a compound such as 3M Imperial Compound or 3M Super Duty Rubbing Compound. If you're using the latter or its equivalent, you'll want to apply it with a buffer at a slower speed and then use a faster speed to buff it in and off while it's still wet. Your buffing pad will become gummy quickly because this is like working with pure liquid clay. Have a spur and extra buffing pads handy.

> **Note:** If you're afraid of ruining your gelcoat when trying different mixes of wax and compound, remember that it's not the mixing of products that typically ruins gelcoat, but rather the incorrect use of a buffer. You can "burn" gelcoat if you (1) use the buffer at too fast a speed when you're buffing off wax or compound that has dried to a haze, or (2) press too hard on the buffer when using a thin cleaner wax or light compound.

Once you have finished the first step of removing the layer of oxidation from the gelcoat, you're ready to apply polish (if you're doing a three-step process) or wax (if you're doing a two-step process). In either case, you can apply the product by hand and use the buffer to buff it off. This will ensure a more even finish. You should use a pure liquid wax for the two-step approach even if you removed the oxidation in the first step, but you can use a thinner product such as Meguiar's or SeaPower rather than a thicker one, like 3M. If your first pass with compound left a perfectly glossy

A waxed and buffed topside. Compare this polished surface with the dull gelcoat in the photo on page 45.

surface, you can effectively apply a soft wax or polish (with no compound in it) by hand or with a buffer.

For a Level 5 Boat (Chalky and Pitted)

If your gelcoat is at this degree of oxidation, chances are you have an older boat or one that sits in the sun and has not been waxed in a long time. An older boat in this condition most likely has thin, worn gelcoat as well. This combination—extreme oxidation and thin gelcoat—is a bad one. In this case your goal is not to bring back a glossy finish but rather, first and foremost, to remove as much oxidation as you can without compounding completely through the remaining gelcoat. Then you'll want to apply a good coat of wax to protect the remaining gelcoat and prevent further oxidation. If this compromise yields a glossy finish, pat yourself and that good ole boat on the back!

Follow the same steps as you would for a level 4 boat. If your boat is older and the gelcoat is fairly thin, however, be careful not to press too hard on the buffer when you're buffing the wax off. Definitely do not work in direct sunlight or on a very hot day, or the wax will soak in almost instantly and be difficult to remove. Do small sections at a time for this same reason.

Waxing Colored Stripes

If your boat has colored stripes on topside or at the waterline, there is a risk that the color will run when waxed, especially if you're using compound or the stripe is older. The best way to prevent this is to apply painter's tape on either side of the stripe. Once you've taped off the stripe, wax it (by hand or with a buffer), then remove all wax dust and haze with a microfiber rag. When finished, slowly lift the tape to remove it. If you are then ready to wax the area around the stripe, apply painter's tape over the freshly waxed stripe and it won't run when you wax that section with the buffer.

A Final Word on Waxing

After reading these detailed instructions, tips, notes, and suggestions, you might still feel like you just don't get it. You might still be asking yourself, "But how exactly do I use the buffer? Where do I even begin?" It can seem overwhelming if you have never done it before, but don't fear or fret because all it takes is simply trying it. Purchase the gear and supplies you think you'll need for your gelcoat's condition. Take it all down to your boat and spread everything out in the cockpit or on the aft deck. You're going to do test spots in this area because it's easy to reach, and it's an ideal place to lay out all your gear for quick use, and it's easy to look at from many different angles.

On 1 foot by 1 foot sections, test various waxes and techniques, by hand and with a buffer. In fact, make this first workday simply a test day, testing everything until you get the result you're looking for. Bring a notebook and write down what's working, as well as a few tips and tricks you learn along the way just by doing. This way, you'll be able to look at those notes to see exactly what worked best instead of wondering what it was you did in the third test square that worked so well.

When working with a power buffer, it's always best to hold the buffer pad flat against the gelcoat rather than at an angle. Holding it at an angle can cause swirl marks. While holding it flat, apply a medium amount of pressure on the machine. You shouldn't just be holding the buffer delicately against the gelcoat, but neither should you be leaning into it with all your weight. Find a happy medium, and that's the amount of pressure you want to apply on oxidized areas.

The buffer will grab and jerk around when the buffer pad gets gummy with wax. If you're buffing off compound or cleaner wax on an oxidized boat, however, you have to buff it off while it's still a little wet, and this will cause the buffer pad to gum up quickly. Keep a spur nearby, and periodically run it through the pad while running the buffer to release the clumps of wet wax buildup. Keep several clean pads on deck so you can change them often when one gets too gummy. A book can tell you only so much about how to wax your boat with a buffer. Every boatbuilder uses a slightly different gelcoat formulation, every boat has a different level of oxidation, and you can never predict the weather, so there's no one way to do it exactly right for all boats. Practice is king!

Don't worry if you feel like your dock neighbors are watching you. They probably are, and they're most likely thinking you know what you're doing simply because you're out there doing it and are hoping to learn a thing or two by watching. Just keep working, and very soon you *will* know what you're doing!

Maintaining a Painted Topcoat on Fiberglass

Many of today's larger custom fiberglass boats and yachts are coated with Awlgrip or another two-part polyurethane paint rather than gelcoat. Additionally, many older fiberglass boats have their decks and hull topsides painted when the gelcoat can no longer be restored with compound and wax. Awlgrip is frequently used in this application, too, but so are other two-part polyurethanes, modified one-part urethanes, and even ordinary marine alkyd enamels (which work fine on wooden boats, though they might need to be renewed each year or every two years, and last longer on fiberglass, which doesn't swell, contract, and work as wood does). I focus here on Awlgrip because I've had the most experience with it, but my comments apply to other painted fiberglass surfaces as well. The bottom line is that painted fiberglass surfaces should not be waxed.

Awlgrip provides long-lasting, high-gloss coverage; has excellent resistance to sun, salt water, chemicals, and abrasion; and doesn't require much maintenance. Over time, however, a buildup of dirt, grease, and other contaminants can dull the finish. This section provides some simple tips to help you keep your Awlgrip looking its best for a long time.

Washing Awlgrip

Whether the finish is gelcoat or Awlgrip, it is best to wash any boat on a fairly regular basis (at least once a month) to help keep water stains, bird and spider droppings, road dust, and other pollutants from setting in. Regular cleaning will also avoid buildup of dirt, grease, and other contaminants, which can cause Awlgrip to age prematurely. This premature aging is what causes the finish to appear dull. Use a soft mitt or brush on the end of a long-handled pole, and rinse it out thoroughly before you start to make sure there are no small pieces of debris (a pebble, grain of sand, or piece of shell) from the last wash that could scratch the painted finish. As for soap, Awlgrip's manufacturer makes a soap specifically for an Awlgrip finish. It's called Awlwash (who would have guessed?), and you can buy it at most boat supply stores or order it online through the company's website.

Awlwash does not contain alkalies, acids, or abrasives, and that's why it's specifically recommended for use on an Awlgrip finish. However, other boat soaps can be used on Awlgrip without hurting the finish. Read the label to check for alkalies or acids, and make sure the label says that the soap is safe for painted finishes. It is best not to use soap with wax in it on an Awlgrip finish. Pour one or two capfuls of soap in a bucket, add water, and you're good to go! While washing, it is important to keep the surface wet and to rinse well to prevent the soap from drying on the surface. You should follow up with a squeegee or chamois to remove water spots, or attach a water filter between the hose and the water source to prevent water spots from forming once the water evaporates.

Protecting Awlgrip

Awlgrip's manufacturer has created another maintenance product, called Awlcare, that can be applied to an Awlgrip finish just as wax is applied and used on gelcoat finishes to remove pollutants, protect the finish, and provide a glossy shine. Awlcare is a hand-applied, non-abrasive, synthetic polymer used to seal and restore gloss to a painted surface dulled by age or mistreatment. It will remove mild stains, water spots, and diesel soot and, when applied regularly, will increase resistance to attack from acid rain and other pollutants. It contains no harsh abrasives and therefore will not scratch the painted finish. Awlcare leaves a non-yellowing, protective polymer coating that lasts through multiple washings. Never apply Awlcare with a machine buffer. It can be removed with Awl-Prep Plus when it's time to repaint.

Traditional waxes are not recommended for use on Awlgrip finishes. These waxes break down rapidly on Awlgrip, and the residue can cause the topcoat to appear yellow—plus it attracts dirt. This creates the need to maintain the wax, increasing overall maintenance. Traditional waxes, which contain no abrasives, probably do little harm to the coating, but neither do they offer any benefit. And when the surface needs to be repainted—as it inevitably will after eight to nine years if not sooner—any wax you've applied will need to be removed before the surface can be sanded and prepped for painting.

Cleaning Marks and Stains on Awlgrip

Over time, marks and stains are bound to appear on your beautiful finish. Black scuff marks from shoes, green marks from hoses, grease, handprints, bird dropping stains, and more will accumulate with time. With a gelcoated boat, you would simply use some cleaner wax to remove these stains, but with Awlgrip, a quick hit with cleaner wax isn't the best solution. Although Awlgrip makes a product (called Awl-Prep Plus) that can be used to remove marks and stains on an Awlgrip finish, it may not be easy to find at your local boating store. In its place, it is possible to use toluene, lacquer thinner, methyl ethyl ketone (MEK), acetone, or kerosene to soften or remove a heavy buildup of grease and grime.

When using solvents to remove stains, test an inconspicuous area first. Apply the solvent with a soft, clean cloth and wipe up quickly. Do not allow the solvent to dry on the surface or puddle and soak into the surface. Afterward, rinse well with water to remove any residue. The above-named solvents are aggressive and toxic and should be used with proper skin and breathing protection. On the less harmful side, you can use distilled white vinegar and hot water to remove stubborn salt stains, but rinse well with fresh water when finished.

Here are a few don'ts from Awlgrip (which you can find on the company's website):

- ▶ Do not use abrasives, magic, or rubbing compounds on an Awlgrip finish. Scratching the surface gives dirt a place to cling while wearing out the resin layer. Using abrasives of any kind will reduce the life of the finish.
- ▶ Do not allow contact between Awlgrip and teak cleaners. Most teak cleaners contain acids or caustic agents that stain and discolor an Awlgrip topcoat.
- ▶ Do not allow metal polishes to dry on an Awlgrip finish because these polishes may discolor and stain the painted surface. Metal polishes contain acids, and rainwater and dew running off metal fittings can spread metal polish residue onto an Awlgrip surface and etch and dull the paint. Washing freshly polished metal fittings thoroughly with soap and water can help eliminate polish residue and reduce the metal polish runoff.
- ▶ Do not allow wet gear (for example, seat cushions, coils of line, sails, sail covers, coolers) to trap and hold moisture against an Awlgrip topcoat. This condition can result in blistering or delamination of the painted finish.

Maintaining an Awlgrip finish may sound like a lot of work, but the main thing to focus on is to wash your boat at least once a month throughout the year and after each return from a saltwater outing. This is the best and easiest way to keep an Awlgrip finish looking good for years.

CHAPTER 3

Teak Decks

If your boat has teak decks, you can appreciate the beauty of honey-colored wood that looks golden when wet or even the distinguished beauty of naturally aged gray wood. Although some people don't mind the weathered look and even prefer it over the golden honey color, if your teak has dark stains from oil, grease, or dirt, it should be cleaned and brightened to maintain the integrity of the decking. This chapter covers the following information on maintaining your teak decks:

- ▶ Why and when to clean teak decks
- ▶ Gear and supplies
- ▶ Preparation and safety
- ▶ Cleaning teak decks—step-by-step
- ▶ Oiling teak decks

Why and When to Clean Teak Decks

You'll know it's time to clean your teak decks when they start looking gray or develop dark stains from grease, oil, or dirt. It's not a serious situation if they start turning gray, but the main thing you're trying to prevent is the actual breakdown of the teak and its

Teak with grease stain

Natural gray teak decks look beautiful when free of grease stains and dirt particles.

underlayer. Older teak decks that are well weathered typically have a more open grain on the surface than newer teak decks. You'll know if the grain of your teak is "open" if you can feel ridges when you run your fingers over it against the grain. You can also see these ridges fairly easily. Consider that if the grain of your teak decks is open, the dirt, salt, and grease that end up on your decks are getting into the grain of the teak. Once those particles have settled into it, it's impossible to get them out without scrubbing, thus opening up the grain even more. And once the grain is opened, it's open for the life of the teak. It does not close up on its own. Preventing this from happening in the first place if you have new teak decks will help them last a lot longer. Maintaining your teak decks is actually quite simple and doesn't take a lot of time if you keep up with them.

Gear and Supplies

There are two main types of teak cleaners on the market—acidic and non-acidic. The non-acidic cleaner usually comes in powder form and is somewhat less harsh on the teak than the two-step acidic cleaners and brighteners. But keep in mind that most of the "harshness" in teak cleaning comes from using a course scrub brush rather than a soft brush or going with the grain rather than against the grain. A soft brush makes all the difference! If there are not a lot of stains in the teak from grease and dirt or the teak is fairly new, try

Note: There are many tips and tricks to cleaning and maintaining teak decks, and you'll find plenty of heated discussions in online boating forums about this topic. That's one thing I love about boats and their owners. They are usually passionate about their boats and how to take care of them. The information I cover in this chapter suggests a few of the many ways you can clean and maintain teak decks; these are by far not the only ways.

using the powder cleaner first. If the teak is older or has several dirt and grease stains, use the stronger two-part solution. But first, let's learn more about what you're actually putting on the decks.

Teak Cleaners and Brighteners

Non-acidic cleaners typically come in the form of a powder that contains an alkaline-based cleaning compound, which is still strong enough to clean light dirt and grease stains and is somewhat more environmentally friendly than an acidic cleaner (or rather the better of two evils). There are also liquid cleaners that don't contain acid and are advertised to do the job of cleaning and brightening in one step. Once again, if you have newer teak or you're unsure about which type of product to use, start with one of the non-acidic cleaners.

The stronger two-part teak solution is made up of Part A (the cleaner) and Part B (the brightener). Using these products is like coloring your hair. Part A (which is acidic) basically bleaches or strips a layer of color from the teak, as well as removing dirt and grease, and Part B—the base—neutralizes that acid. When acids and bases are mixed together, they react to neutralize each other if an equal number of hydrogen and hydroxide ions are present. When this reaction occurs, salt and water are formed.

The two-part teak cleaning and brightening system for older teak

$$HCl + NaOH = NaCl + H_2O$$
(Acid) + (Base) = (Salt) + (Water)

This is why it is so important to rinse the decks thoroughly when you are finished working with Parts A and B. A combination of applying the acidic cleaner and scrubbing the teak will slightly open the teak and allow crystals to embed in the decks if they aren't thoroughly rinsed. It's also why it is better not to clean and brighten teak decks in direct sunlight. The decks can dry too quickly and sun can cause any type of crystal (from salt or other chemical residue) to burn or etch into the teak, causing discoloration or a breaking down of the material or fibers over time.

There is no need to list specific product brands in this category because all boating supply stores carry teak-cleaning products. Your main decision is whether you're going to use a one-step cleaner (usually in powder form), a one-step cleaner and brightener (liquid form), or the stronger two-step cleaner and brightener (always in liquid form). Once you've chosen the product, the next step is making sure you have the right brushes.

Brushes

The right type of brush makes all the difference. Think of teak cleaning and brightening as attacking your innocent teak. It didn't ask to be drenched with chemicals or temporarily discolored. It was fine just sitting there on your boat, protecting your fiberglass decks and preventing you from slipping while walking from one end of the boat to the other. And if the chemical cocktail of teak cleaner wasn't enough, it's about to get scrubbed with a brush to help spread those chemicals about its surface. (It's not the teak's fault that your tipsy non-boater friends chose to drink their red wine on your beautiful teak or that Duke with Duke's Engine Repair and Mess Making didn't take off his greasy boots before crossing the teak deck to the engine room.) The least we can do is not open the grain of the teak any more than it might already be, thus exposing the wood to more elements and particles that will further break it down over time.

You'll need three types of brushes when working with teak. The first is a long-handled pole with a soft deck brush attachment, the same kind you would use on smooth gelcoat. This is the main brush you'll be using to reach most of the deck. The second is a small hand brush with soft bristles. This brush is used for hard-to-reach places where the deck brush can't fit. The third is a small hand brush (think of a large toothbrush) with medium-course bristles that aren't stiff or feel like plastic. This is the brush you'll use to scrub the edges of any teak where mildew has formed. Use this brush lightly and try to go against the grain rather than with the grain when you scrub.

> *Tip:* Remember, a brush is soft enough for gelcoat, plastic windows, and teak if it doesn't scratch when you run it across your face.

The only other cleaning gear you'll need is a hose, nozzle, and bucket. But before starting, consider that you'll be working with chemicals no matter which type of cleaning product you've chosen. This warrants a quick discussion about preparation and safety.

Preparation and Safety

Before you use these products, either the acidic or non-acidic formula, there are several important steps you need to take to protect you and the gelcoat from harsh chemicals.

First, let's protect you. When you start to brush these cleaners on your decks, they are going to splatter, so make sure you're wearing rubber boots. The chemicals in both solutions can stain clothing, so also make sure that you're wearing an older pair of pants or your rain gear so you don't ruin a good pair of jeans. This is definitely not the project to do quickly before your dinner guests arrive at your boat. And most importantly, wear rubber gloves. You will know if any of the chemicals get on your skin because they will sting or burn badly until you wash them off. It's always a good idea to protect your eyes when working with any type of chemical, so if you have protective eyewear, you should wear it.

The next thing you want to protect is the gelcoat near the teak decks. While brushing the cleaners over your decks, areas near the teak will get splashed or sprayed with the chemicals, which can stain gelcoat if they're not hosed or wiped off.

Using chemicals to clean teak decks is a project that you'll do only once or twice a year, so make a point of doing it after you wax your boat. This way, the chemical overspray will sit on top of the coat of wax and not "soak" into the gelcoat. If the gelcoat isn't waxed or you have an Awlgrip or other type of painted finish, have an old rag handy so you can wipe the splashed gelcoat clean while waiting for the chemicals to do their job on the teak. Use that rag to also wipe any stainless steel or other metal finish that gets splashed with the chemical cleaner to keep it from staining or etching the metal.

> **Note:** While you're working, you'll invariably get some of the chemical solution on your rubber gloves (which is why you're wearing rubber gloves), but be careful not to accidentally scratch your head or face while you're working. And if your cell phone rings, let it go to voice mail! Spreading these chemicals around on your skin or your cell phone will only remind you of how badly they burn and sting!

Plan to do this project on a cloudy day or even on a day when it's misting or raining very lightly. You shouldn't clean and brighten your teak decks on a very hot day or in direct sunlight because you don't want the chemical to dry out on the teak while you're waiting for it to do its work (usually about a three- to five-minute wait). And mist or light rain will wash the chemicals off the gelcoat for you.

Cleaning Teak Decks Step-by-Step

If you have new teak decks, the best way to keep them clean from the start is to wash them when you wash your boat. Use the same long-handled pole and deck brush that you use when washing the smooth gelcoat on your boat, as well as the same soapy water from your bucket that you used on the rest of your boat. Absolutely do not use a scrubbing brush or anything you wouldn't use on your smooth gelcoat or plastic windows. A rough brush will open the grain of the teak, and that's when problems can arise. Another natural way to maintain clean teak is to wash it with seawater using a soft deck brush. The salt in the seawater helps the teak to retain moisture and stops it from shrinking away from the caulking. But don't just dip your bucket into the seawater at the marina because any oil, fuel, or other contaminates that are seeping out of nearby boats can leave a residue on your teak and turn it darker and darker over time. If you're going to wash with salt water, wait until you're under way on a cruise; then carefully scoop a bucket of fresh salt water to throw over your decks.

If you plan to use a chemical solution, prepare for that treatment in the following ways, no matter which product you'll be using. Turn the hose water on at your slip and bring the hose to the area where you'll be working. Wear rubber gloves throughout the whole process. Grab your long-handled pole with a soft deck brush attached, as well as a soft hand brush for hard-to-reach areas. Your goal is to have everything you need to do the job ready and with you. You don't want to have started brushing Part A teak cleaner about your teak decks only to realize that you left the hand brush on the dock box. You'll end up tracking the chemical on all other surfaces you walk on, which means more cleanup and work to keep it from discoloring teak or staining gelcoat.

Open all the bottles of solution so they are ready to pour or squirt. (You may need scissors or a utility knife to cut off the tops of the Part A and Part B bottles of the two-step cleaner and brightener.) Once the chemical solution hits the teak, you'll want to work fairly quickly (with the deck brush and the hand brush you've assembled) to spread the solution around. You'll also want to make sure to corral the solution so it doesn't run down the sides of the hull, and lightly hose any cleaner off the gelcoat before it discolors it.

> **Note:** If you want to clean and brighten a teak ladder or steps that are over a teak deck, do the steps first. The chemicals will drip down onto the teak deck, which is fine because you'll eventually be cleaning and brightening the deck below. If you do the steps after the deck, you will stain the deck with the chemicals that drip down on it and have to redo it. Be sure to apply the teak product on all sides of the step for an even-finished look.

You're now ready to start. Hose down all the teak that you'll be cleaning, as well as the gelcoat and metal near that area. Generously sprinkle the powder or squirt the Part A cleaner over a section that's about 6 feet by 6 feet. Set the bottle down, then take your long-handled pole with the soft deck brush and lightly scrub over the area, going against the grain. Remember, you are not trying to scrub hard because the chemicals are doing all of the work. Your job is to simply deliver those chemicals to every inch of the teak by spreading them about with your soft deck brush. Once you have covered this 6 x 6 section, start on another 6 x 6 section while the chemicals do their work on the first section (about three to five minutes, depending on how old or stained your teak is). Both the powder and the Part A cleaner will turn the teak a dark cherry red and some areas will become pulpy. That's the result we're looking for, so don't let it worry you.

Once you've spread the powder cleaner or the Part A cleaner on all of the areas you want to clean, take your hose and spray it off. Consider that the chemical will be running out of drains or openings and may run down your hull. To prevent staining, every now and then lean over the rail and spray down the hull in any areas where the chemical comes in contact with the gelcoat.

Use a soft deck brush to spread the product, and always go against the grain.

Tip: If you have a lot of teak area to clean, halfway through your work, take the hose and lightly spray over the first sections you worked on. You don't want the chemical to dry on the deck (especially the powder cleaner) because it could be difficult to remove or cause permanent staining.

If you used the one-step non-acidic cleaner, you are finished with your work for the moment. Take a look at your decks once they've had a chance to dry and see if they look any cleaner (no grease or dirt stains) or if they are honey colored. If they are only a little cleaner or there are still several dirt and grease stains, your decks are ready for the stronger acidic two-step process the next time you schedule this project. Wait a few weeks before treating the decks with the stronger cleaner/brightener solution.

If you're using the two-step process, it's time to squirt the Part B brightener solution onto the decks. Some two-step teak-cleaning products tell you to squirt the Part B brightener solution onto the decks after applying the Part A cleaner solution without hosing it off in between; others suggest that you hose off the Part A solution before applying the Part B solution. I suggest the latter, for two reasons. First, the Part A solution is a chemical, and the longer it sits on any material (wood, gelcoat, metal), the more damage it can do. Second, I have found that there is less chance of causing light and dark streaks in the wood if you hose off most of Part A before applying Part B. Another way to avoid streaks in the teak when applying the Part B liquid is to pour it in a basket and dip the brush head in there instead of squirting it on the teak.

Take the same precautions as you took with the Part A cleaner because both solutions contain chemicals that you don't want touching or soaking into your skin or the gelcoat. With your teak decks still wet from being hosed off, squirt the Part B solution in 6 x 6 sections, using the soft deck brush to work it in, going against the grain. Let each section sit for three to five minutes, but don't let it dry. Lightly spray water over any section that starts to dry before you're ready to hose off the entire deck. If you see that the wood has turned a light honey color, the brightener is doing its job. Hose the decks thoroughly, and remember to hose the side of the hull if there is any runoff in that area.

If the edges of the teak decks are green with mildew, you can take the mildly course scrub brush and go over the edges lightly with the brush, scrubbing against the grain. If that doesn't remove the green mildew, spray mildew cleaner over the green area and use a soft hand brush to work it in. Rinse well with water when finished.

Alternative Teak-Cleaning Methods

Use a mildew spray and a small scrub brush to remove mildew on trim pieces.

In my years of working on boats, I have learned that all you have to do is walk down the dock toting the highly acidic Part A in one hand and the alkaline-intense Part B in the other hand for boaters on your dock you didn't even know existed to pop out of the woodwork and pull you aside to tell you what they've been using on their teak decks for the last 97 years.

I gave you step-by-step instructions on how to use the more aggressive two-step teak products above because most people will use them at one time or another and those products require the most skill. When using acidic cleaners, there isn't much time before mistakes can be made. But there are several alternative methods for cleaning teak that work very well. If you have newer teak decks, I would not recommend the acidic cleaners because you don't need them and they'll be too strong for your tight-grained teak. If you clean your teak decks on a regular basis using less aggressive methods, your teak's grain will do its job better.

The alternative method I cover here is simply using soap and water to clean your teak decks. Soap comes in different strengths, and the kind you use will depend on the condition of your teak. If the teak is brand new or still golden in color, wash the decks with the same soap, water, and soft deck brush that you used to wash the rest of the boat. Remember to go against the grain so you don't risk opening up the grain; that is always the main thing you're trying to prevent no matter what method of teak cleaning you use.

If your teak decks are showing some gray or there are oil stains in places, try a stronger soap. I recommend Cascade dishwashing liquid with bleach (if you

An alternative teak-cleaning method for newer teak

moor your boat in a gray-water marina). Pour some in a bucket (start with a few cups to see how far it goes), then spray just enough water in the bucket so the dishwashing soap is not as thick. Wet the decks with the spray. Use the long-poled soft deck brush to thoroughly mix the soap solution, then spread it over the entire deck, going against the grain. Then go back to where you started to see the results. If the decks look lighter and more golden, hose off the decks. If they seem to need a bit more time, let the mixture sit on the decks for a few more minutes, then hose it off. This soap-and-water method should leave your teak decks lighter and brighter without having used a more aggressive product.

Oiling Teak Decks

To oil or not to oil, that is the question—and there is no incorrect answer. You can leave them honey or gray without oiling them, and the woods' natural oil will protect them, as long as you keep them clean and quickly remove grease or dirt by washing them when you wash the boat or using the cleaner/brightener system once or twice a year. Using teak oil will give them a deep honey color, but they will still require regular maintenance in addition to several extra post-cleaning steps to prepare for oiling.

If you have decided to oil your teak decks after cleaning and brightening them, you will need to gather a few additional items to start your project. The list includes:

- ▶ Blue painter's tape
- ▶ Cotton rags
- ▶ Sandpaper (150 grit)
- ▶ Paintbrushes
- ▶ Plastic container
- ▶ Work gloves and knee pad (for comfort and to prevent splinters)

It's time to start preparing the teak, assuming that your teak decks do not need repair work before you coat them with oil. If there are chips in the wood or places where the wood has separated from the caulking, then repair work on those areas should be done before you apply oil. If you are uncertain about doing this yourself, you should contact a brightwork or teak specialist to do the work for you. Whole books could be written (and many have been) on how to repair or resurface teak decks. Because my specialty is detailing rather than repair work, I gladly leave that topic to an expert in the field.

Start by sanding the teak with sandpaper to smooth out any ridges, but don't sand so hard or so much that you remove all ridges to a perfectly flat finish. Because oiling your teak decks necessitates sanding every time you do it, which could be every few months in sunnier climates like Florida or the Caribbean, that's a lot of sanding for the life of the decks, even if it's only every six months in a less sunny location. Your goal with sanding is to take out the most extreme ridges and leave a slightly smoother finish on the grain.

Once you have finished sanding, hose the decks down thoroughly and let them dry completely. If you don't have time for this, at least vacuum the dust out of the grain. Use painter's tape to tape off anything that shouldn't be oiled, such as metal fittings and stanchions, gelcoat, and varnished wood rails. However, this is why you should keep cotton rags handy, in case you need to quickly wipe teak oil off something it wasn't intended for.

You might find it easier to decant the teak oil from the bottle it came in to a plastic container for easier dipping with a paintbrush. Then use the brush to paint the teak oil on the deck, going with the grain. Avoid getting the oil on the caulking. Wipe it off with cotton rags as you go. "Paint" your way off the boat, then allow the teak oil to soak in and cure completely so it is no longer wet or tacky. All teak oil is slightly different, so see what length of dry time the manufacturer recommends on the bottle. One thick coat is enough and should last three to six months depending on your climate, how much you use your boat, and where it is moored. Obviously if it is moored in a sunny climate or salt water or you use your boat often, the teak will need to be re-oiled every few months for a perfect finish. If you have a covered slip, don't use your boat as often, or moor it in fresh water in a not-so-sunny climate, a perfect finish should last a bit longer.

CHAPTER 4

Brightwork Maintenance

Don't varnish it. Don't oil it. Just paint the rails brown. End of story. Now, let's get back to the game. Oh, you did that last year, you say? Well, let's see if we can't come up with some maintenance tips and advice to help keep your wood protected and looking good. This chapter is mostly about varnishing wood, but it does mention a few other types of coatings for use on exterior wood. I divide this chapter into a few easily digestible sections. This chapter covers:

- ▶ Comparing exterior wood finishes
- ▶ Determining the condition of your current finish
- ▶ Gear and supplies
- ▶ Preparation and safety
- ▶ Getting started sanding and varnishing
- ▶ Caring for varnished wood

Comparing Exterior Wood Finishes

There are several different ways to care for the wood on your boat, including everything from covering it with mul-

Some boaters varnish rails and some leave them natural.

tiple coats of varnish to leaving it bare. The following is a brief comparison of the most commonly used exterior wood finishes.

Varnish

Most everyone loves the look of glossy varnish on a boat's rails and trim. It's what gives the boat that timeless look of a traditional seafaring vessel. Maintaining that look, however, takes more time than most people have. The decision to varnish exterior wood is balanced by the protection it offers versus the ability to maintain it on a regular basis so it can do its job.

Varnish is typically made up of five ingredients, which include oil, resin, solvent, dryers, and ultraviolet additives, all of which have an effect on how long the varnish will last and how well it will protect the wood from the elements. Here's a list of these ingredients to give you an idea of what to look for when shopping for exterior varnish.

- ▶ Tung oil is commonly used, which provides long-term resistance to cracking and crazing. The main purpose of tung oil is to improve penetration into the wood; the more oil in a varnish, the better the penetration.
- ▶ Resins, which are derived from natural sources (tree stumps or crude oil), help varnish dry faster and give it a hard finish that is more resistant to water and other elements.
- ▶ Solvents aid in the leveling process of varnish. They help varnish lie down on the wood, so brushstrokes are not as visible.
- ▶ Driers simply help accelerate the drying time and improve the hardness of the coating.
- ▶ Additives are used in varnish to improve the finished cosmetic look and make the varnish last longer to protect the wood. Different additives that may be used include anti-skinning agents, flattening agents (typically used for interior varnishes), and ultraviolet additives so that any UV light entering the coating is diffused back.

Most varnishes contain all of these ingredients, but some higher quality varnishes take it a step further and provide longer-lasting protection. Interlux Goldspar Clear or Schooner 96 varnishes use three different additives to combat UV light. An ultraviolet absorber (UVA) reflects most of the light away from the wood; the remaining UV rays that are not reflected back are dispersed evenly throughout the coating so there is no single attack on the film. A surface stabilizer works at the surface to repair damage from UV light. By keeping the surface film repaired and stabilized, the amount of water, which can attack a broken paint film, is reduced, prolonging the life of the coating. Antioxidants are the third additive; they are used to combat photodegradation and the effects of oxidation on the varnish film. Without an effective antioxidant, the varnish will gradually fade and become cloudy. With any clear coating, like varnish, it is particularly important to maintain its color because any change will be readily detectable. (This information is from the Interlux website—www.interlux.com.)

Two-Part Catalyst Systems

For boaters who don't have the time, energy, patience, and perfect weather, and who don't love sanding as much as they thought they would, there are now several two-part varnish products on the market that allow you to apply all the coats in one weekend. These two-part catalyzed urethane coatings include Honey Teak (by Signature Finish), Bristol Finish, and Perfection Varnish (by Interlux).

These varnishes can be used on bare wood or wood that has been varnished previously and simply needs new coats built up. The products contain a catalyst that cures the resin into a highly durable surface, and their molecular cross-linking ensures a perfect bond between coats with little or no sanding and a much faster dry time, so you can apply the next coat in just one to two hours. These catalyst systems look the same as varnish when dry and have additives just like varnish that protect against UV rays, abrasives, and chemicals coming into contact with the finish.

The slight downside to using these types of products is that you have to follow the instructions very carefully in preparing the mixture of the urethane base with the catalyst. And because these products are thinner than varnish and don't have the leveling agents that varnish does, you have to apply them more carefully and mind your brushstrokes. You cannot just "slap it on" as you can with varnish because they won't level as well as varnish will. Because this chapter mostly discusses the application of varnish, you should use the instructions provided with the two-part system if you plan to use this type of coating for your wood. All of these companies provide detailed instructions that are easy to follow, and they have helpful and convenient phone and Internet support.

Oil

Oil, such as tung or linseed oil, is easy to apply (just wipe it on with a rag or use a foam brush) and gives the wood a deep, rich color (the oil darkens in sunlight). But because it penetrates deeply into the wood, leaving less of a surface finish, it doesn't do a very good job of actually protecting the surface of the wood, and it allows UV rays to do damage over time. In most sunny climates, oil usually lasts for less than six months and requires re-coating several times a year to effectively protect the wood.

Synthetic Finishes

These types of finishes (such as Cetol, by Sikkens) are like your Uncle Clem who lives in a van down by the river—strong, but not always the most attractive choice. If you don't mind the color of pumpkins, Cetol has many benefits: it lasts a long time, it's very durable on exterior wood, it offers UV protection, and it's easy to apply and maintain. If your rails are already coated with Cetol and are in good condition, then by all means simply maintain the finish with a few new coats throughout the year (more often if you're in a tropical or sunny climate), and maybe even apply Cetol Overcoat to give the rails a glossy finish. After an initial sanding, you can apply several coats of Cetol without sanding in between coats, waiting only 24 hours or less to apply the next coat.

Epoxy

I don't go into much detail about epoxy because a book specifically about brightwork would cover this topic in full. However, using epoxy on bare wood before applying varnish offers many benefits, especially in the way that it seals wood and protects it from water. Some of the companies that offer epoxy resins are West System and Interlux. The following benefits and uses of epoxy resins as suggested by West System include:

▶ Using a resin and clear hardener as a base can give your brightwork a richer look while protecting it longer without having to apply as many coats of varnish.

▶ Because there are no solvents evaporating away from the epoxy, it builds thickness faster per layer than varnish and it doesn't shrink when it cures.

▶ Sealing wood with an epoxy moisture barrier dramatically lessens its stretching and shrinking, helping the varnish last longer because it's on a stable surface.

▶ Undercut the wood trim around all edges by ¼ inch and glue the edges down with epoxy to eliminate places where water can get in.

▶ Apply epoxy to screw holes prior to running the screws in place to prevent water from seeping in.

Determining the Condition of Your Current Finish

Assuming that you are planning to apply varnish as opposed to another type of finish and that you are working with bare wood or previously varnished wood, the next step is to determine the condition of the wood and the condition of the current varnish. It is not you who will make this decision, but rather the wood that will determine what you need to do—build up more coats, patch-coat it, or take it down to bare and start anew. The following "cheat sheet" can help you decide which of the three options your wood requires.

▶ If the wood still has a solid covering of varnish (no areas of bare wood or discoloration) but has simply lost its gloss, the varnish is simply thinning and all you need to do is build up new coats of varnish on the wood.

▶ If you can see small areas of bare wood through the current varnish or areas where the wood has turned dark gray or black, or the varnish has become discolored around stanchions and other metal parts, you can iso-

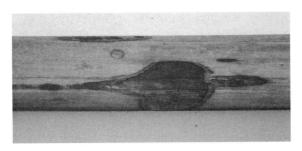

Old varnish—black water stains and peeling varnish

late these problem areas with tape and then patch-coat them.

▶ If the current varnish is peeling or blistering, the underside of the rails feels rough or has been worn down to bare wood, or the current varnish has yellowed or looks faded, the varnish has gone too long without proper maintenance and is no longer protecting the wood from harmful UV rays, salt spray, or water. In this case, it's best to take the wood down to bare and apply new coats of varnish.

Gear and Supplies

The following gear and supply list includes everything you might need to varnish wood in any condition. The better the condition of your wood, the fewer items you'll need.

Different options for hand-sanding hard-to-reach areas or curved-rail edges

▶ **Sandpaper.** It's best to buy several different grits, ranging from 50 to 320.

▶ **Sanding block or sponge.** A sanding block helps you sand more evenly over a long, flat surface; sanding sponges help you sand curved areas.

▶ **Scrapers.** Buy a couple of different sizes; scrapers with rounded corners are preferable. While you're buying scrapers, grab a file to help keep them sharp.

▶ **Tape.** Use painter's tape so it comes off easily. Do not leave it on longer than a few days, especially if it has rained. (If you do end up with tape residue on the fiberglass, apply 3M Adhesive Remover with a rag to take it off.) Taping off where you're working prevents varnish from getting on the gelcoat and prevents you from scraping the gelcoat with the sander or sandpaper.

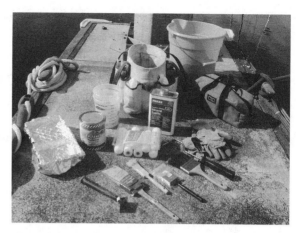

Varnish gear

▶ **Tack cloth or microfiber cloth.** These cloths will grab any surface dust or particles sitting on top of the wood. Use them just before applying varnish.

▶ **Denatured alcohol, acetone, or MEK.** Use denatured alcohol to wipe down wood just before you apply varnish. Use acetone or MEK to remove varnish drips that land on other surfaces.

▶ **Brushes.** Look for quality brushes meant for varnish. The last thing you want are little brush hairs coming out of a cheap brush and drying in your smooth varnished rails.

▶ **Tarp or drop cloth.** Lay out a tarp or drop cloth and put all of your gear on top of it rather than directly on your decks or nonskid. The tarp will contain the inevitable spills and drips, as well as any sharp objects. It also gives you a specific area to place gear and supplies, which makes it easier to find things and much easier to clean up.

▶ **Plastic containers.** These are ideal for decanting varnish from its original large container so you can more easily hold it in one hand while you move about the boat. Plastic containers are also handy for holding used brushes, rinsing out brushes, and holding small screws and other hardware that you may have had to temporarily remove.

▶ **Finishing sander.** If you have large areas of flat wood, a sander will quickly become your best friend. Not only does it speed up the process, it can sand the wood with more even pressure than your fingertips can, and it will be easier on your hands and wrists for large jobs.

▶ **Chemical stripper.** I don't recommend chemical strippers simply because they're toxic to the skin and lungs. However, they do the job, and they're useful for removing varnish from large areas or areas that are difficult to reach or fit into with a sander.

▶ **Bleach or oxalic acid.** You'll need one of these products to remove water stains from the wood.

▶ **Heat gun.** A heat gun is a good way to strip old varnish without using chemicals. You'll need a scraper to remove the varnish while holding the heat gun near it.

▶ **Vacuum cleaner.** You may want to bring a shop vac down to the boat to remove any sanding dust in the area where you've been working. A breeze can pick up quickly and scatter that dust onto the fresh varnish you just applied.

▶ **Band-Aids and aspirin.** Need I say more?

Preparation and Safety

Planning Your Time

In varnishing, preparation is king! It will take you one-tenth the time to actually apply the varnish; all the rest of the time will be spent preparing your gear, supplies, and wood. In fact, preparing for and applying multiple coats of varnish can take up to several weeks. With this in mind, if you don't have this kind of time and patience or enough perfect weather, you may want to consider the two-part catalyst urethanes.

Preparation is 90 percent of the job.

Whichever type of finish you choose, preparation is still the most important part. For example, if you have a full Saturday and part of the following afternoon to work, then use all of Saturday to prepare the wood by setting up your gear, sanding the wood, and completely cleaning up your work area. The following afternoon, use a tack cloth or denatured alcohol to wipe down the wood to remove any dust or other dirt particles that landed since you left, then apply a coat of varnish. Of course, your schedule, the weather, and collecting or buying all the gear and supplies you'll need may not always work out as easily as that, but it's a good way to start planning for this project.

Safety

Safety is also king, and it's something to take very seriously when doing this project. I cannot stress this enough—wear a face mask whenever you're sanding! If that fine dust gets into your respiratory tract, it will cause your lungs to physically hurt. You should also wear thin latex (or similar) gloves when working with varnish, chemical stripper, bleach, oxalic acid, acetone, or MEK. (However, don't wear gloves of any sort when working with a heat gun.)

Weather and Other Conditions Beyond Your Control

Before you race down to your boat to slap a few coats of varnish on the rails, take a minute to check the weather conditions. Avoid applying varnish if there is a chance of rain, strong winds, or extreme hot or cold temperatures coming your way. Read the label to learn what the ideal temperature range is for that particular varnish. Some varnishes are fine to apply in direct, hot sunlight, while others will become too sticky or runny in those conditions. (If the forecast is for hot sun for weeks on end, add a thinning agent to the varnish to prevent it from going on too thick.)

Look around to see what's going on near your boat. Especially on a breezy day, make sure your dock neighbors aren't washing their boat, doing fiberglass repair work, or waxing their boat. If you know your varnish project is going to take several days or weeks (as it most likely will), and you use a detailer to wash your boat on a regular basis, make sure you let them know about your project so they don't show up to wash your boat minutes after you've left for lunch while the varnish is drying.

If you moor your boat next to a bridge that cars travel over, you may want to consider moving your boat to a slip for a few weeks that is farther away from the bridge, or to a different marina altogether. You will not be able to achieve a perfectly smooth finish if road debris and dirt particles are constantly settling on your varnish, even if there is no wind.

Getting Started Sanding and Varnishing

Just as you should spend more time on preparation than actually applying the varnish, this chapter spends more time on what you need to know before picking up the brush than instructing you on exactly how to do the work. Once you've determined the condition of your wood and decided which process you're going to take, bought all the supplies and set them up on your boat, and checked the weather and planned your schedule, you are now ready to begin doing the actual work. This section will help you get started and give you the basic guidelines you'll need to effectively complete the job. However, you might want to read a book written specifically on brightwork, such as *Brightwork*, by Rebecca Whitman, which goes into complete detail about all the steps, tips, and tricks you should be aware of when embarking on this project, especially what to do when you run into problem areas. Also read the product instructions carefully because some manufacturers may have specific steps you must take in a given order or disclaimers you should know about the product you're using (for example, what temperature it works best in or how long it takes to cure).

Also, if you have never varnished wood or worked with a sander, you should practice on something other than your rails or name placard because any mistakes will easily be seen in those areas. Try sanding and varnishing your bread board, or purchase some small pieces of lumber (preferably the same type of wood as on the boat you'll be varnishing) that you can practice on.

Building Up Coats

If your current finish isn't showing signs of wear and tear and you simply want to build up more coats (which is recommended every three to nine months depending on your climate and conditions), you have a fairly straightforward job ahead of you.

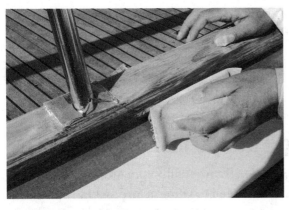

Use a soft block to sand between coats.

1. Lightly sand (by hand or with a sander) the current finish with 240- or 320-grit sandpaper. You can also use a red or green Scotch-Brite pad. Your goal is to lightly scuff up the current finish and remove any gloss so the new finish will adhere to it.

2. Brush or vacuum off the sanding dust, then wipe the wood with denatured alcohol to remove any fine dust or particles.

3. Apply a fresh coat of varnish with a bristle or foam brush or a roller.

4. Allow to dry (usually 24 hours, but read the label first to see how long it takes to cure), then repeat steps 1 through 3 until you have built up the desired number of new coats.

Patch Coating

If there are only small areas of bare wood or water stains and the rest of the finish has a nice sheen or solidly covers the wood, you can get away with patch-coating those areas. Follow these steps to fix those problem areas:

1. Outline the area with painter's tape.

2. Use 180- or 220-grit sandpaper to sand that area down to clean, bare wood. Always wear a face mask when sanding wood.

3. If there are water stains (where the wood is black or gray), use bleach or oxalic acid to remove the stains. Simply rub it on with a rag or apply with a foam brush to saturate the area, then wipe it off with a damp rag or rinse with water. Be sure to wear protective gloves.

4. Let the area dry and then use fine-grit sandpaper (240 or 320) to sand the wood in preparation for varnishing.

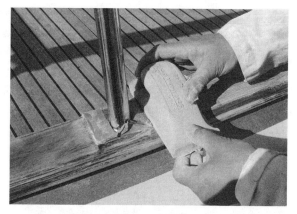

5. After sanding, wipe down the area with denatured alcohol, and vacuum or sweep away any sanding dust.

6. Apply one coat of varnish to the area using a bristle or foam brush.

Sand right up to the stanchions so this area is better protected from water seeping through.

7. Most finishes require you to let each coat dry before lightly sanding with 320-grit sandpaper and applying the next coat. Repeat until the repaired area matches the rest of the wood.

Taking It Down to Bare

The current finish on your wood is no longer doing its job if it's peeling, blistering, or fading or if there are several areas of bare wood or water stains. Follow these general steps to take the wood down to bare and apply new coats of varnish.

Old varnish that is peeling—it's no longer protecting the wood and is causing water stains

1. To protect the gelcoat, use painter's tape over the gelcoat where it abuts any wood you'll be sanding.

2. Completely remove the current finish by using one or more of the following methods: a sander or hand sander, a heat gun, a scraper, or a chemical stripper. If you want to use a mix of everything available to you, apply a chemical remover to loosen the old finish, let it sit for several minutes (read the instructions on the label), and rub it off with a 3M or Scotch-Brite pad. You may have to repeat this application a few times depending on how many old coats of finish are on the wood. Wear gloves and a face mask anytime you are working with strong chemicals. Follow the chemical remover with a scraper (and a heat gun, if needed, but only after you have removed all of the chemical stripper) to remove old strips of varnish that are still sitting on the wood. They'll come off fairly easily thanks to the chemical remover, so be careful not to push too hard on the scraper, and make sure the scraper blade is sharp so your work is accurate. Once you've reached bare wood and 90 percent of the old finish has been removed, use an electric sander with 180 grit to sand the entire area. Repeat with 220-grit sandpaper.

Use a heat gun and scraper to remove old varnish on trim and smaller areas.

3. Check the phone book for a varnisher who is (a) affordable and (b) available in the next six months to fix the gouges from the scraper and the burn marks from the sander. (Sorry, I don't mean to assume the worst. I'm sure you're doing just fine and are not frustrated at all and are looking forward to twelve more continuous hours of sanding before the rains come.)

A rail sanded down to bare wood

4. Decide if you need to use any wood fillers or epoxy to fill any uneven areas or fill a seam where two pieces of wood meet to better protect that area from water seeping in. Let the filler or epoxy dry completely before sanding smooth.

5. Now, follow steps 3 through 7 above under "Patch Coating." Your goal should be to build up at least four coats of varnish, but more if you have the time and opportunity.

Of course, when you look at the actual condition of the wood on your boat and notice all of the small trim pieces, the ornate designs in the wood, and the number of stanchions you have to tape and varnish around, these steps aren't going to seem as simple as they do on paper. The key is to not rush through it. Plan to do one section at a time and figure out a realistic schedule that works with your free time and the weather.

Caring for Varnished Wood

Once you've finished this project and you have beautiful varnished wood, your next step is to actively take precautions that will keep it looking that way for as long as possible. The best way to protect varnished rails is by having canvas covers made for them and keeping the covers on except when you're cruising or enjoy-

A hose or power cord can easily scratch varnished rails.

ing the boat in its slip. Having custom canvas covers made can be expensive, but the added protection they give your varnished rails will make a huge difference in how often you have to refinish the wood.

You can use wax on varnished wood for the same reasons you would use it on gelcoat—to protect it from harmful UV rays, clean it, and seal it. Use a pure carnauba paste or liquid wax that contains no rubbing compound. Apply a light coating with a small, round foam or terry cloth wax applica-

tor pad (available at any boating supply store or a store that sells auto detailing products). Let it dry to a haze and then wipe it off with a clean, dry microfiber rag. Water will now bead up on the varnished wood, so it will be protected from and help repel salt spray.

When washing your boat, be careful about pulling the hose over any varnished rails because this can easily scratch the varnish. Instead, run the hose under varnished rails. Or, if you have varnished toe rails, secure a cotton rag or towel over the rail where the hose will come in contact with it. This is another reason why having canvas covers on your rails is a good idea—to prevent the hose from scratching or marring the finish.

CHAPTER 5

Interior Cleaning

Cleaning the interior of your boat is similar to cleaning the interior of your house, but in a much tighter space and most likely with a lot more nooks and crannies. This isn't the most exciting chore you'll want to tackle on your boat, but a clean interior can result in a much more comfortable experience when entertaining guests or staying the night on your boat. The best way to tackle this chore is to make sure you have a working radio nearby and some rubber gloves. Both will help you get through this project unscathed! This chapter covers:

- ▶ Deep cleaning versus maintenance cleaning—when and why
- ▶ Gear and supplies
- ▶ Deep cleaning
- ▶ Maintenance cleaning
- ▶ Hiring a cleaning service
- ▶ Organizing for small spaces

Deep Cleaning Versus Maintenance Cleaning—When and Why

Twice a year, preferably in spring and fall, you should do a deep cleaning on your boat. The rest of the time, a maintenance cleaning should suffice. What exactly is a deep cleaning? It's when you actually lift up the seat cushions, look under things, and use your Q-Tips and old toothbrushes so you can clean every inch of the interior. A maintenance cleaning is when a rag and a spray cleaner will do most of the work. If you haven't cleaned the interior of your boat in a while, a rag and spray cleaner won't get the interior truly clean or smelling fresh. You first need to tackle the problem areas the way only a deep cleaning can do. This may require a full weekend, so be prepared to set aside some time to complete this task. It may also require a few trips to the dry cleaners or hiring a carpet cleaning service. Deep cleaning isn't difficult work, but it can be somewhat tedious and requires an eye for detail. A radio program playing in the background or help from a talkative friend will make the job go much faster!

A maintenance cleaning is something you should do after each cruise, or once a month if you're not using your boat often. Even if there's no one around to see it, dust still happens! So does mildew growth and stale smells caused by moisture in the air. A maintenance cleaning is where you'll dust or wipe down all surfaces and check for mildew or other growth in the head area. If you check often enough, you'll catch any sort of growth before it becomes a problem and causes more work and musty smells. Also, if you do a maintenance cleaning to the interior of your boat once a month, you'll most likely also catch anything unusual during winter or rainy months, such as water leaking through a window. You'll be able to catch and correct a problem like this before it causes more extensive cleaning or repairs.

Gear and Supplies

A lot of the gear and supplies you'll use to clean the interior of your boat can come from your own arsenal of house cleaning supplies (this is the one place where it's all right to use household products on your boat). Before you leave the house, assemble the following items to take to your boat. If you don't have these on hand, you can buy them at any grocery or variety store and won't have to make an out-of-the way trip to your local boating-supply store on your way to the dock. Besides, boating-supply stores carry a limited selection of cleaning products for use on interior surfaces, and they charge much more for them.

- ▶ Garbage bags
- ▶ Rubber gloves
- ▶ Multipurpose spray cleaner for counters and windows (such as Windex or SprayWay)
- ▶ Spray cleaner for grease (such as 409)
- ▶ Mildew spray cleaner without bleach

- ▸ Orange oil wood cleaner/conditioner (for use on real wood paneling only)
- ▸ Murphy Oil Soap (for use on wood floors)
- ▸ Portable vacuum cleaner with attachments (if your boat doesn't have a central vacuum system)
- ▸ Microfiber rags
- ▸ Paper towels
- ▸ Scrub brushes

Also, wear older clothes that are easy to move in. You'll be dealing with hard-to-reach places and standing in odd positions trying to access the far corners of interior storage compartments. Bring rubber gloves to protect your hands from chemicals.

> **Note:** Before you start cleaning, organize the items in the boat cupboards, bookcases, drawers, and shelves so you can easily and thoroughly clean those areas. Bring a plastic container to hold the contents of a shelf so you can clean it, then easily put those items back.

Deep Cleaning

Before you can do successful maintenance cleanings on your boat, a deep cleaning is a necessity. If you don't remove and clean damp and musty cushion covers from the seat cushions, no matter how often you spray and clean any other area of the boat, your entire boat will smell musty and stale. So, let's start with possible problem areas first, then move on from there.

If every time you board your boat, your nose wants to run and hide because of that good ole boat smell, you need to find the source of the odor and take care of it. If you don't, it won't go away. You can cover up those musty or stale smells with Febreze for only so long before you realize that the source of the odor may actually be serious or may be causing respiratory problems, as in the case of mold or mildew. I assume you have had the heads pumped out recently, but if you haven't and you detect a strong smell (one that you can't mistake for any other), have the heads pumped out. Once you're able to rule this out, try to locate the source of the musty smell. Most likely it will be from damp bed linens, curtains, towels, cushions, or other fabrics. Once fabric becomes damp, which can happen from a long, wet winter (Seattleites know what I'm talking about), mildew starts to form in the fibers of the material. You may not see it, but you'll be able to smell it easily, and the fabric may even feel cool or damp to the touch. If this is the case, mildew is definitely the culprit, or at least one of them. Remove the fabrics, linens, or cushions from the boat, then go back into the cabin to see what else you can smell. Carpeting typically won't be the problem unless you know for a fact that water soaked the carpet at one point and it never had a chance to fully dry. Also check the bilge areas; water can pool under the floorboards. Lift up the floor hatches and pump out any water or soak it up. When there's no water left, spray Simple Green or 409 in that area and do a final wipe-down with paper towels.

Take all fabrics and removable cushion covers home and run them through the washer and dryer. You don't need to put them back on the boat until you plan to use the boat again, so if it's fall or winter when you do this, and if you don't use your boat much in the winter, put the fabrics in a container and store them at home until you need them on the boat. Take cushion covers that are part of the cushion and can't be removed to your local dry cleaner, rug cleaner, or commercial fabric cleaner. They will be able to clean and dry your cushions better than your own washer and dryer at home. Ask them to treat the cushions with a stain guard as well.

Your boat should now be free of bedding, cushions, towels, and curtains, which will make all of those areas easier to clean in and around. The next step is vacuuming up all of the crumbs, dirt, dust, and other things you've dropped from the last boating season, so you'll have less to wipe away. When starting an interior cleaning job for one of my customers, I vacuum every surface from top to bottom. You'd be surprised at how much easier it is to spray and wipe these areas once you've vacuumed up most of the dust and dirt. And if spiders inhabit your boat, your vacuum will easily get rid of them.

While vacuuming, lift up anything that lifts up, such as bench seats and storage hatches. Vacuum shelves, bookcases, sinks, and cabinets. Use the small vacuum attachment that fits into tight places, and use the brush attachment to go over the walls, wood paneling, and headboards. Your goal is to vacuum up most of the dirt and dust so that one pass of a rag with spray cleaner is all you'll need to get that area shiny again.

Do a thorough job of emptying out your storage compartments. Chances are, you'll find old cleaning products in there that may be leaking or old metal containers that have become rusty. If you had put anything away wet or damp, it may have mildew on it, and that could be one of the sources of the moldy odor. This is a good time to throw away old products and containers and inventory what you have in your storage compartments. Most likely you won't need all of those items, so keep only those you use on a regular basis, and store the rest at home or in your dock box.

The galley and the head are other areas on the boat where you'll want to spend extra time doing a deep clean now so that maintenance cleanings in the future are actually effective. Open all fridge and freezer doors and com-

Tip: It's always a good idea to clean the interior of your boat with as many windows open as you can or even a fan blowing. With the mix of mildew, chemical spray cleaners, and dust in the air, you'll need all the fresh air you can get while you clean. If the smell is too strong for you at times or you feel lightheaded, take a break, step outside, and breathe fresh air for several minutes to clear your lungs and head.

partments and empty them if possible. If any water is pooled in the freezer, sop it up and make sure to dry it thoroughly. If there is mildew in the fridge or freezer, spray those areas with mildew spray cleaner and let it sit while you work on another area of the galley. Open the compartment where you store garbage and remove any full garbage bags or containers from the boat. Check around the garbage container to make sure garbage didn't miss the container and fall near it. Spray this area with a bleach spray cleaner. This type of cleaner kills bacteria, eliminates odors, and even removes tough stains.

Go back to the fridge and freezer and use paper towels to wipe the mildew off the interior surfaces you've just sprayed. I suggest paper towels instead of microfiber rags because they can be discarded. Mildew isn't something you want to take home along with rags destined for the washing machine. Once you've wiped all mildew off the surfaces and from the crevices with paper towels, you can then use a microfiber rag and a multipurpose cleaner to clean the rest of the compart-

ment. If you don't plan on using your boat soon, turn off the power to the fridge and freezer and prop the doors open. Put a container of baking soda in each to freshen the interior and control moisture.

The head is the other area that definitely needs deep cleaning. Once again, vacuum inside the cupboards and storage compartments and around

Tip: When you dry microfiber rags in the dryer, don't use any type of fabric softener. It will destroy the rags' ability to absorb water. Without fabric softener, they'll have a lot of static and will cling to one another (you'll have a shocking time pulling them apart fresh out of the dryer), but they will be the softest and most absorbent rags you can use for cleaning the interior and exterior of your boat.

the toilet. If the shower floor has a wood grate, lift that up and vacuum under it. Vacuuming will remove 80 percent of the dirt, hair, and grime you would otherwise have to clean by hand. If the head is extra dirty or hasn't been cleaned in a long time, spray some orange room freshener in this area. Wear a face mask to make this job a bit more pleasant and easier on your senses.

Once you've thoroughly vacuumed all areas of the head, empty out cupboards and items in the shower and throw away old products that you no longer use or containers that are leaking. This is where you have to get down and dirty. It's time to don your rubber gloves (if you haven't already), crank up the radio, assemble your cleaning arsenal, and go to town! Use the bleach cleaner in places where it won't run down a drain (don't use any type of bleach cleaner in the toilet). Bleach, although a very effective cleaner in the head area, will dry out PVC pipes and tubing, causing them to break down or crack over time. Clean the toilet with a marine-grade toilet cleaner that you purchased at the boating supply store. This is the one area (involving drainpipes) where you don't want to use household cleaners.

Use the bleach or antibacterial cleaner spray to disinfect the shower, around the toilet, and on counters. Use it on the walls around the toilet where toilet water has splashed and made water spots. Use a window cleaner for mirrors, windows, and shower doors. Use a multipurpose cleaner along with a scrub brush to clean the floors of the head and the shower (if it's a nonskid material) and inside cupboards. If you have a shower curtain that has become stained or mildewy, now is a good time to replace it. Once you are finished with this first pass of deep cleaning, go over all surfaces again with a microfiber rag and multipurpose cleaner. This will ensure that you have removed all dirt, as well as any residue left on surfaces by the stronger cleaners.

Clean just as you would at home, but avoid products with bleach.

If the interior of your boat has wood veneer paneling, use a microfiber rag and multipurpose spray cleaner or Murphy Oil Soap and spray lightly over the wood, then wipe it clean. If you have real wood paneling (you can tell if it's real wood as opposed to veneer by the exposed grain, which you can feel), use orange oil wood cleaner/conditioner spray and two microfiber rags—one to wipe off the orange oil spray and one to lightly go back over all of the wood you've cleaned to remove any oil residue. As the initial rag you're using to wipe off the spray becomes saturated, use less orange oil spray. A little bit goes a long way.

Spray the orange oil on a section of wood and wipe it over the grain. Instantly, your wood will shine and any areas of wood that are discolored or scuffed will blend in with the rest of the wood. You will get overspray on the floor, so if you have a wood floor, be sure to wipe off the overspray well or it can get quite slippery. After you wipe down the wood-paneled walls, clean the wood floors with Murphy Oil Soap to remove the overspray completely. Do not use orange oil spray cleaner on wood floors because it will make them too slippery. When you finish wiping off your first pass of orange oil spray from the wood-paneled walls, use the other microfiber cloth to wipe all of the wood. The cloth will soak up any oily residue and leave the wood grain with a perfect and even shine.

It's best to save carpet cleaning for last because you'll be walking all over your carpets while you clean, and any overspray of cleaning products will land on them, which will only attract more dirt. Start with a thorough vacuuming of all carpeted areas. Once you remove all loose dirt in the carpets, you'll be able to see any stains, marks, or spots that need to be treated. If there are only a few small spots or stains, treat them with a carpet spot cleaner such as Folex, available at most grocery or variety stores. If there are several spots and stains, it's best to use a professional-grade carpet cleaning machine rather than trying to spot-clean all of them. This is because spot cleaning will make that one spot look extra clean against the rest of your possibly faded or slightly soiled carpet.

Keep after carpet stains as soon as they occur.

If your carpets are beyond spot cleaning (and it doesn't take much for them to fall into this category), it's best to rent a carpet cleaning machine or have a carpet cleaning company professionally clean them with the right

> *Tip:* If your boat is used often, yet you want to preserve its carpets for future resale value, install carpet runners that snap to the floor. Any canvas service company can measure and install them for you. Then, a few times a year, simply pull them up and clean them in your home washer and dryer. Use a low heat setting when you dry them so they don't shrink.

products and techniques. This is something you may want to do once a year to keep your carpets looking their best.

Maintenance Cleaning

If you have recently deep-cleaned your boat's interior, maintenance cleaning will be that much easier and more effective. It can be done quickly and easily after each outing. All you'll need is a vacuum cleaner, a few microfiber rags, and a multipurpose spray cleaner. First, vacuum all areas, especially heavily used areas such as the head, galley, and carpets. Then use a multipurpose spray cleaner and microfiber rags to spray and wipe all surfaces. If you did a thorough deep cleaning recently, you won't need to lift every bench seat or hatch or bother cleaning every cupboard or drawer. You also won't need to wipe down all of the wood unless you know of a specific area where something was spilled and it touched the wood. A maintenance cleaning is also a good time to:

Microfiber rags are a great way to quickly clean or dust any interior area.

- ▶ Empty the trash and put a new trash bag in the garbage can.
- ▶ Empty the fridge, freezer, and cupboards of half-eaten foods, half-full beverages, old food, and food other people brought that you have no intention of eating.
- ▶ Squirt a marine-grade toilet cleaner and freshener in the toilet.
- ▶ Spot-clean carpet stains that occurred recently.

Hiring a Cleaning Service

After reading all of this and realizing you'd rather be doing pretty much anything this coming weekend than deep-cleaning the interior of your boat, you may decide to hire a boat detailing service that offers interior cleaning, or a house cleaning service. A boat detailer will know how to turn the power on and what types of products to use or not use on your boat. A house cleaner may not. If you decide to use a house cleaning service, it will be in your best interest to remain on or near the boat most of the time to help answer their questions. You'll need to let them in the boat, show them where the power is (or, better yet, have all light, outlet, freshwater, and head switches turned on for them), help them get the power back when their high-amp portable vacuum shorts a circuit, and show them how to turn the lights on and off and how to flush the head. If you can afford it, the best situation would be to find someone who can clean the interior of your boat on a regular basis and eventually get to know your boat so you don't always have to be there.

Use microfiber rags to clean all stainless.

And how often is often enough? I would recommend doing a deep cleaning every spring, then follow it up with maintenance cleanings after each outing or at least once a month. In fall before you stop using your boat as often, do a light deep cleaning, empty the fridge and freezer, and remove all seat cushions and bedding.

Organizing for Small Spaces

I can't tell you how many times I've been cleaning the interior of a boat when I've opened up a cabinet or closet, only to have all of the items that were stuffed in there come spilling out onto the counter or floor that I just wiped down. We all know that storage compartments, closets, and cupboards on boats usually don't offer nearly as much room as we need to store all that we want to keep on board. But there are ways to make the most of the space you have, keep it better organized, and make it easy to put things back in their proper place. Here are a few tips and tricks to make storing gear and supplies a little easier.

Storage Containers

Clutter must be contained, and the best way to do that is with plastic containers that you can label. Whether you need them with a lid or open on top, handles or no handles, holes or no holes will depend on where they're going and what they will be used for. Before you run out and buy tubs and bins, look through the items you have in the storage areas of your boat and note which ones you should store

A well-organized storage compartment makes it easier to find things and keep clean.

together (for example, all games, decks of cards, and puzzles for the kids can go in one place) and what size container you'll need for them. Make a note about each type of container so when you go to the store to buy them, you'll know exactly what you need.

Small storage containers, trays, or bins are an ideal way to organize the items you keep in drawers. Just like a silverware drawer, you don't want all of your utensils sliding around; using a silverware tray makes it much easier to keep the utensils organized so you can easily find what you need. Likewise, you could use a similar system for other drawers.

For example, if you keep a flashlight, batteries, and small tools in a drawer, organize them in bins so it is easier to find what you need when you need it. Nothing will have slid to the back of the drawer, and it will be much easier to clean the drawer or reorganize where you keep things because you need to lift out only one or two bins rather than seventeen batteries, five screwdrivers, and thirteen bits. In addition, if one of the items in that drawer leaks or can mark something, keep those items in a container to prevent permanent stains in that drawer. Remember, when you someday go to sell your boat, you want it to look as clean and new as possible. When prospective buyers open up each drawer to look inside, the last thing they want to see is the ink from a broken pen soaked into the wood or the sticky residue from candy with crumbs stuck to it. I see this all the time, and ink stains are very hard to clean and usually don't come out completely.

In the Galley

The galley is the best place to use small storage containers for food items and baking products. Many boaters keep their flour, salt, sugar, and other baking ingredients, as well as snacks like nuts and chocolate chips, in Ziploc bags. This is a fine way to store ingredients that would otherwise take up more space in their original packaging. But keep these filled Ziplocs in an airtight plastic bin or container; they will stay fresh longer, and if the Ziploc bag hasn't been zipped all the way or has a hole in it, the inside of the container will be much easier to clean than the inside of a storage compartment or hard-to-reach shelf.

Also remember that boat interiors can get damp in the wet, cooler months. This is another reason why airtight containers are an ideal way to store food items. In fact, you might even take this a step further and rethink the way you store spices. Moisture in the air causes spices to clump and lose their flavor and freshness. When cleaning galleys, I'm always amazed at the vast number of old spices stored in a drawer or cabinet. Go through your spice drawer or cabinet and remove any that are old or clumpy or not used very often. To save space, buy spice blends rather than the individual spices to make the blend. Keep the spice jars in a tray or container with low sides so you can remove the whole thing from a drawer or cabinet and set it on the table for everyone to choose from. Cleaning the tray or container is much easier than cleaning out spilled spices or spice "crumbs" from a drawer or a cabinet that is up high and hard to reach.

Keeping toiletries in small containers in the head will greatly decrease the amount of time it takes to clean shelves and cabinets—especially when you have a drippy toothpaste tube or a shampoo spill—and will help you keep things clutter-free. Keep a container with holes in the bottom in the shower with shampoos and soap. This way, everything is contained, but the water will drain through the holes. Keep all seasickness remedies in their own container so they are quickly accessible and guests on your boat can find them easily. Since toiletries can be messy if they leak or spill, this is definitely one area where keeping these items in handy containers will make cleanup and organization much easier.

In your house or on your boat, a junk drawer shouldn't exist, just as the category of "miscellaneous" shouldn't exist when organizing items for storage. It's just too abstract, and eventually everything ends up in the junk drawer. If you find that you don't have a place for something, you may not need to keep it on the boat, or you may not need it at all. Make the decision right then and there to throw it out or take it home with you (or give it to your dock neighbors and let them figure it out). It's the small random objects collected over time that start to pile up in drawers for lack of a better place to put them (like the garbage can). They can drive you mad the day you sell your boat, when it takes you seven hours to remove all of those miscellaneous items from the far corners of each drawer and clean up after them.

When you can look in each drawer, closet, and cabinet and clearly see exactly what's in it, can easily clean that area and quickly remove containers to empty out your boat, you will feel less "cluttered" and more organized and in control of your space. Take these organizational tips outside and use them to organize exterior storage spaces where you keep cleaning products and bottles of oil or other greasy liquids. This is a good way to prevent spills from dirtying the nonskid or seeping into the teak decks, and it makes cleanup in that storage compartment much easier and faster.

 **6**

Canvas, Carpet, Vinyl, and Plastic Windows

Keeping your boat's furnishings clean and well maintained adds to your own enjoyment of the boat and also helps increase or at least keep its value in the long run. Pay attention to the details of canvas covers and enclosures, curtains and other interior fabrics, interior and exterior carpet, vinyl seats and cushions, and plastic windows to keep these materials looking like new. This chapter covers:

- ▶ Canvas
- ▶ Plastic windows
- ▶ Outdoor deck carpeting
- ▶ Interior carpet
- ▶ Vinyl seats and cushions
- ▶ Interior fabrics

Canvas

Choosing and Buying Canvas

If you just bought a new boat and you're planning to purchase canvas covers or enclosures for it, here are a few things to consider before you buy. Canvas covers and enclosures are expensive, so buy them from a company that will come to your boat, measure thoroughly, use a test pattern to make sure the final pieces fit, offer you choices and options, and answer your questions.

If you have not purchased canvas covers and enclosures before, think about what color will look good on your boat, and still look good when it's been on your boat for several years and starts to fade or become dirty. White and light tan will show the dirt much faster than dark colors, but black isn't a good option because it causes heat and humidity to build up inside the enclosed area, which foster the growth of mildew. Medium shades of blue or green (as opposed to navy or pale blue and hunter or light green) tend to look newer longer and don't cause as much heat buildup.

You'll also want to decide what type of system to use to secure the canvas enclosure to your boat. The two main systems are metal snaps or hooks and loops. With metal snaps, a female snap is sewn into the canvas and a male snap is screwed into the fiberglass. With the hook and loop system, a plastic hook is screwed into the fiberglass and an elastic loop is sewn into the canvas every 12 inches or so. The hook and loop system is preferable to metal snaps for the following reasons. Over time, canvas—originally measured for a tight fit—can shrink slightly from constant wetting and drying in rain and sun. Even slight shrinkage can make it extremely difficult to snap the canvas back into place after it was unsnapped. Also, some airflow is desirable in the enclosed area. The tighter the fit of the canvas, the less airflow under it, which eventually causes mildew to grow because the underside of the canvas stays wet longer. Even a small amount of airflow will help dry the underside of the canvas and deter the growth of mildew. Lastly, with the hook and loop system, you can use a deck pole to reach a loop on the far side of your boat and stretch it over the hook. You can't do that with the snap system because you have to apply pressure on the snap in order to snap it down.

Gear and Supplies

You'll need a few specific items to clean and protect your canvas from dirt, mildew, bird droppings, and other stains that can soak in and ruin the look and the protective properties of the canvas. In addition to a hose, nozzle, and bucket, make sure you have the following gear and supplies before you get started:

- ▶ Long-handled deck brush with a soft brush attached
- ▶ Soft hand brush
- ▶ Small course scrub brush (looks like a very large toothbrush)
- ▶ Mildew spray cleaner such as Lysol or Tilex without bleach
- ▶ Color-safe bleach (available at grocery stores) or Krazy Clean (available at boat supply stores)

Cleaning Mildew in Canvas

Brand-new canvas can make a boat look new again, but it doesn't take long for new canvas to start showing dirt and signs of wear. Although you can't control the weather and other external elements that attack your canvas, you can take steps to keep it clean, protected, and looking good for a long time.

If your canvas tops and covers are new, don't wait for their corners to turn green with mildew before you start cleaning them. Now is the time to put them on a regular maintenance plan just as you should with the exterior of your boat. Every time you wash your gelcoat with a soft deck brush, use the same brush on the canvas. You don't need to use any cleaners other than the soap and water that's in your bucket. This will take off the top layer of dirt. If there are several bird droppings in one small area, you can spray them off with the high-pressure setting on your nozzle. This simple procedure will keep the canvas clean for a long time. If your boat is moored in a wet climate (and it's not in a covered slip), it's especially important to prevent and treat mildew when it starts to set in. And it will set in—because mildew loves canvas, or rather the "ecosystem" that canvas creates.

You know the hot, humid air that hits you when you enter a canvas-enclosed flybridge in the middle of summer. I've always thought an enclosed flybridge would be an ideal place to grow tomatoes. Even in winter, the temperature in an enclosed flybridge is considerably warmer than the outside temperature, especially on a sunny day. In this "greenhouse" atmosphere, mildew grows easily and quickly. You'll first start to see a thin layer of it on the underside of the canvas "ceiling." If you let it go, you'll then start to see green mildew sprouting in the interior seams and rolled edges of the canvas. Finally, you'll see it growing on the exterior seams and eventually on the vertical panels. It doesn't take much to prevent mildew from taking over the canvas, and if you stay on top of it regularly, you may be able to prevent it from growing at all.

Treat mildew in canvas as soon as you notice it.

The best defense against mildew is to prevent it with a good mildew spray cleaner applied every few months. If you live in a dry climate, mildew may not be a big issue for you, but if you live in a climate that is often wet or humid, fighting mildew on a regular basis will be necessary in order to maintain the integrity of the canvas and keep it looking good. You'll find a few brands of mildew spray cleaners at your local boating store, but these are expensive and actually don't work as well as those you'll find at the grocery store. Two of the best mildew spray cleaners are Lysol and Tilex. Avoid the bottles that say "with bleach" on the front label so you can use them on colored materials and not have to worry about discoloration. Mold Off also works well and helps prevent mildew for several months.

Here are a few precautions to take when using mildew spray cleaners. Make sure to wear rubber gloves. The chemicals in these products are fairly strong and will irritate your skin on contact. Also, try to work in a well-ventilated area. If you're treating mildew inside the flybridge enclosure, open some side panels to get a cross breeze. If at any time you feel lightheaded or develop a headache, stop and take a break in fresh air. When you're working on the underside of the canvas "ceiling," some mildew spray drips or mist may float down on you. Wear a face mask and sunglasses or safety goggles.

The only other items you'll need are a soft hand brush, a scrub brush with a narrow head (looks like a very large toothbrush), and a long pole with a soft deck brush attached. If mildew is growing on the underside of the canvas top, the easiest way to remove it is to squirt the mildew spray cleaner on the head of the soft deck brush attached to the long pole. (Wet the deck brush first so it can better absorb the mildew cleaner.) Run the wetted brush over the underside of the canvas, spraying more mildew cleaner on the brush every few strokes, until all of the mildew is gone. You do not need to wipe it dry or do anything further. In fact, leaving a small amount of the mildew cleaner residue on the canvas will not discolor it and it will continue treating the mildew for several weeks without you having to do anything more.

The seams and rolled edges of the canvas often attract mildew faster because the material around the edges and zippers is thicker and doesn't dry out as fast. Also, mildew often grows between the seams sewn in the plastic around the zippered areas. This mildew can be impossible to remove if it's not treated on a regular basis because there is no way to clean that area with a brush or spray unless you take out the seam and restitch it. So, spray the mildew cleaner over the seams and let it soak in or slowly drip down into the seams. For easier-to-reach seams and rolled edges,

Cleaning mildew out of canvas

spray the mildew cleaner over those areas and let it soak in for a few minutes. Then take your small scrub brush and scrub these areas until you see the mildew loosen and dissolve. The mildew cleaner will do most of the work to eat away the mildew, but it is up to you to remove it from the canvas when you're finished. You can do that by cleaning the treated area with a damp rag or hosing it off.

Mildew that has formed on the exterior side of the canvas covers may require more work. This mildew grew when the canvas was wet, but it has since dried on the canvas from warm or dry weather. If the mildew looks more like moss, it will need an even stronger treatment. Spray the mildew cleaner generously on all areas of the exterior canvas that show mildew growth. Then take your soft deck brush or hand brush and work the mildew cleaner into the canvas. Let it soak in for three to five minutes. You may need to repeat this several times before you see any changes. After letting the cleaner soak in, use the soft deck brush to redistribute it all over the canvas again. Then spray off the cleaner with a hose. To prevent mildew from quickly coming back in those areas, lightly spray more mildew cleaner over the canvas but don't scrub it in or hose it off. Leaving it there won't do any damage and will deter mildew growth.

These steps will be most successful on mildew that is green because green mildew is still somewhat "fresh" and new. If the mildew on your canvas is black (this can be difficult to tell on dark-colored canvas), it means that the mildew has been on the canvas for a long time, has dried into it, and has discolored the fabric.

You can try treating the canvas with the steps above, but it may be more beneficial to take the canvas to a commercial cleaner.

Cleaning Dirty Canvas

Over time, canvas that isn't washed on a regular basis will get dirty, especially in areas where water runs over the canvas in the same place every time it rains, or where water pools on the canvas for long periods of time. Before using chemical cleaners and a lot of elbow grease, remove the canvas (such as canvas covers on vinyl seats or benches or canvas covers on ski boats) and put it in your home washer and dryer or take it to a laundromat. Wash it in warm (not hot) water, and set the dryer to low heat to prevent shrinking the canvas. During the wash cycle, add a small amount of waterproofing solution, which is available at camping stores. When drying, throw several dryer sheets in with the canvas covers. Dryer sheets that prevent static cling also help fabric resist water, so rainwater will bead up slightly on the canvas rather than soak into it.

If it's not easy or convenient to remove the canvas covers and launder them in a washer and dryer, you can treat them on the boat with spray cleaners. A mix of bleach in a bucket of water wiped over the canvas with a soft brush will work well, but make sure it's color-safe bleach, even if you have white canvas. I have seen bleach, and cleaners with bleach in them, discolor white canvas, turning it a dull yellow. Krazy Clean (available at boat supply stores) is good at removing water stains from canvas, although a commercial cleaning product might be necessary for water stains that have been there for a long time. If you're going to use a spray cleaner, such as Krazy Clean, Lysol, or Tilex, directly on the canvas, spray it on the brush and then wipe it on rather than spraying it directly on the canvas. This will help to prevent yellowing.

If your boat is moored in salt water or you take it out on salt water often, you know how important it is to wash the salt from the windows and gelcoat on your boat. It's just as important to scrub the canvas to remove all salt spray so it doesn't get "burned" into the canvas and start breaking down the fabric over time.

Plastic Windows

The material used for the plastic windows (also known as Strataglass or Isenglass) on dodger or flybridge enclosures is a special type of vinyl called pressed polished sheets or pressed poly. The material is actually two layers of non-colored vinyl laminated together under intense pressure and high heat. This process squeezes out all the impurities and renders the vinyl perfectly clear. Pressed poly is known by its gauge: 20 gauge is made from two 10-gauge pieces heated together; 40 gauge is made from two 20-gauge pieces heated together, and so on. Like all vinyl, clear vinyl contains plasticizers to keep it soft and pliable and UV stabilizers to retard UV degradation. Over time, if not cared for, clear vinyl can lose its plasticity and become brittle and yellowed, and eventually crack or become hazy and difficult to see through. Additionally, the UV protection added in the manufacturing process breaks down over time, leaving the vinyl with no more UV protection after only a couple of years.

There are several ways to care for plastic windows from the moment you purchase them new to trying to bring them back if they are lightly scratched and hazy. This section explains what items you'll need to clean and protect plastic windows, along with how to do it step-by-step.

Gear and Supplies

The one item you will need no matter what condition your plastic windows are in is microfiber towels. This is the only type of rag soft enough to not leave scratches. Make sure you remove any tags on the microfiber rag so they don't scratch the clear vinyl. Also, keep the microfiber rags you use for plastic windows separate from the rags you use on other areas of the boat or your house. This will prevent the residue from other cleaners not intended for clear vinyl to get on your plastic windows.

The next item you will need is a cleaner spray. There are many good "plastic window" cleaner sprays on the market, but, to be safe, you should purchase one at an auto or boat supply store. You do not want to use a cleaner that contains chemicals that cause drying or hazing. Windex, although a good product for glass windows, should never be used on clear vinyl windows. Some good cleaners specifically for plastic windows are:

- ▶ Meguiar's #17 Mirror Glaze Plastic Cleaner
- ▶ IMAR Strataglass Protective Cleaner
- ▶ Plexus Plastic Polish
- ▶ Mer-maids Plastic Cleaner

If your plastic windows are older and scratched, try removing the scratches before you apply the polish. In the same area of boat supply stores where you'll find plastic window cleaners, you'll also find products that remove scratches in clear vinyl. The products I use most often for this task are 3M Finesse It Finishing Material or 3M Imperial Compound and Finishing Material. These are light compounding agents that don't contain wax. They are excellent for removing scratches and swirl marks and, although they are rubbing compounds, they won't further scratch your plastic windows.

The last product you'll want to have on hand is a polish or sealer. Your first step (using a cleaner) removed dirt. The second step (using a light compounding agent) removed scratches. This final step is where you apply a polish that will help your clear vinyl to resist scratching, maintain softness and flexibility, improve UV protection, repel water, and create an antistatic finish. Some recommended polishes include:

- ▶ Meguiar's #10 Mirror Glaze Clear Plastic Polish
- ▶ IMAR Strataglass Protective Polish
- ▶ 303 Aerospace Protectant

Cleaning, Scratch Removal, and Polishing

If you have new plastic windows with no scratches, all you'll need at this point is a cleaner spray and a polish. If there are light scratches in the plastic windows, use a scratch remover before polishing them, but you'll still start with a cleaner as your first step. Spritz the cleaner spray all over the plastic windows and then wipe it off the entire window with a microfiber rag. If the windows are very dirty or dusty, you may want to repeat this step to get all of the dirt. It's best to wipe down the windows two times lightly than one time hard to prevent possible scratching. If it's a warm day or you're working in direct sunlight, do smaller sections so the product doesn't dry on the plastic before you can wipe it off.

If there are light scratches or hazing in your plastic windows, pour a quarter-size dab of finishing compound on a microfiber rag. Rub it into a small section, preferably in a corner or less noticeable area of the window. Rub it until the liquid product starts to dry, then wipe it off with another microfiber rag. This should remove light scratches and minimize deeper scratches and hazing. If this step worked to remove the scratches or hazing, continue working the product into sections of the plastic windows until you have covered all areas. If it's not working, it's because the scratches are too deep, the vinyl is too old, or the hazing has already done too much damage and has been on the window for a long time.

After cleaning the plastic windows and trying to remove scratches and hazing, you are now ready for the final step of polishing the clear vinyl to improve its resistance to dust, dirt, scratching,

Use only microfiber cloths to clean plastic windows.

hazing, and water spots. Some polishes come in a spray bottle and some are a liquid paste that you apply as you would wax. Spray the polish on the plastic window or pour some onto a microfiber rag. Work it into the plastic, wiping it on evenly and covering all areas. If you've wiped on a liquid paste polish, take a clean microfiber rag and lightly wipe it off. If you sprayed the polish on and wiped it off, you may want to take another clean microfiber rag and go over the windows one more time without adding any polish to make sure you wiped off all of the residue.

It may be difficult to reach the outside of the plastic windows with a microfiber rag. I sometimes drape a rag over my deck brush to reach these areas. If you have a very soft deck brush attachment for a long-handled pole, you can use it sparingly to wash any hard-to-reach window panels as long as you use plenty of soap and water and rinse quickly and thoroughly to prevent the soap from drying and water spots from forming.

If you clean and polish your plastic windows once every month or two, they will continue to perform as they were intended—a clear protective window at the helm station, pliable window panels that you can roll up to allow airflow throughout the flybridge, and an enclosure to keep the weather out while cruising or enjoying your boat at the slip.

Outdoor Deck Carpeting

Outdoor deck carpeting on your boat provides a more comfortable area to walk on with bare feet and for little ones crawling around on the aft deck. It makes your boat feel more "homey" and gives it a finished look. The best places for deck carpet are on the aft deck (or sundeck), the stairs leading up to the flybridge, and the cockpit or flybridge itself. I don't recommend putting carpet on the swim platform because it will always be wet and you'll always have to scrub it to remove any mildew. When it's wet, it can also be slippery, and that's the last thing you want as people board your boat.

Types of Outdoor Deck Carpeting

There are two main types of outdoor deck carpet—berber and pile. Berber looks like small hooks or loops, and pile consists of very close-trimmed fibers much like carpet you might see in an office. Outdoor carpet manufactured specifically for marine use is produced from solution-dyed fibers enhanced with UV stabilizers to protect the carpeting from salt water and extreme sun and moisture.

One very important factor about deck carpeting for your boat is that it must stay in place! You want carpet with a rubber backing, or you'll want to install snaps around the edge of the deck and the carpet to snap the carpet into place. From a cleaning perspective, snapping carpet is the smarter choice simply because if you don't take up the carpet occasionally to clean the deck underneath or put it away for the winter, over time the rubber backing can "melt" into the nonskid and make a mess when you finally take up the carpet. The backing can also dry out and become brittle, so when you pull up the carpet, the dried-out rubber cracks into hundreds of small pieces, making a mess on your nonskid deck.

One type of carpeting not to use on a boat is throw rugs. They are not made for harsh marine environments and will often bleed or shed on the nonskid when wet. If left in place for a long time, the nonskid will become discolored where the rugs were lying. And because they can move around easily, they're not safe.

If you want to have throw rugs made for high-traffic areas to use when entertaining or while docked at the slip, request a few throw carpets to be made by the company that makes your deck carpet (or look in your local boating yellow pages for a carpet company). Make sure the throw rugs are backed with rubber so they have a good grip on top of your deck carpet, but put them away when they're not in use so they remain in good condition and the rubber backing doesn't affect your main deck carpeting.

If you are going to have work done to your boat, put away the deck carpets and bring out some rubber work mats or plastic sheeting (available at larger hardware and variety stores) to protect your nonskid carpets from grease, oil, nicks, and stains during the work. This is especially important if workers will be in the engine room!

If friends will be on your boat, definitely put the carpeting down. Most non-boaters don't always choose the best shoes to wear on a boat, and carpeting allows someone wearing heels, shoes with poor traction, or shoes with black marking soles to feel safe and comfortable walking around while still protecting your nonskid. (This assumes you actually have non-boater friends!) If you have teak decks, you might put custom deck carpets down when you entertain. Unfortunately, there's not much you can do about your guests spilling their red wine or ketchup, except to keep the carpet cleaner nearby!

Gear and Supplies

Here are a few items you'll want to have on hand for cleaning carpet stains and preventing stains from soaking in.

- ▶ Carpet stain remover, such as Folex or Spot Off
- ▶ Carpet stain guard, such as 3M Scotchguard
- ▶ Mildew spray cleaner, such as Lysol or Tilex
- ▶ Hand scrub brushes

Keeping Carpet Clean

Keeping your outdoor deck carpet in good condition isn't difficult as long as you're proactive about keeping it clean and dry. If someone spills something on it, wipe it up as quickly as possible. Better yet, spray your carpets with a stain guard to prevent stains from soaking in. Keep a carpet cleaner spray and scrub brush nearby to get a stain out when it happens.

Pull your carpets up in the wet winter months and keep them in dry storage. This will give them a much longer life than if you keep them on your boat year-round. Even if your carpeted sundeck is covered or enclosed, wet weather can cause dampness in an enclosed space (think of your sundeck like a greenhouse) and foster the growth of mold and mildew. Additionally, if rain drains in such a way as to touch the edge of the carpets at an entryway to your sundeck, for example, the carpet edges will rarely have a chance to dry out and will surely turn green with mildew.

What to do once your tan carpets have turned green? Buy a mildew spray cleaner and spray it on the carpets and scrub it in with a brush. You can then hose off that section, provided the carpet will get a chance to dry. If not, simply use a little less spray, but work it in well and leave it in the carpet. It will continue to treat the mildew and prevent it from coming back.

Leave the mildew spray cleaner in the carpet so it will keep working.

If you left your boat carpets down all winter and they're looking green and dingy, take advantage of the first warm days of spring or summer to give them a thorough wash. Take them off the boat and lay them on the dock, then spray them with a carpet cleaner or mildew spray cleaner (if needed) and scrub them with a light bristled brush. Let the cleaner sit for a while, scrub it again, and then hose it off. Lay the carpets out to dry and then put them back on the boat for the warmer months.

If your deck carpets are looking dingy and spot cleaning just won't do the trick, or you don't want to spend your free time cleaning your deck carpets, take them to a carpet cleaning company to do the job for you. However, there will come a time when even the most professional carpet cleaner won't be able to revive the softness and color that once existed—for example, on carpets left on the deck for the past twelve winters. In that case, it might be time to get new deck carpeting. This is a good time to switch from a rubber-backed carpet to a snap-on carpet, to choose a new color, and to start keeping the carpeting as dry and clean as you can.

Maintaining deck carpets is not the most exciting part of owning a boat, but boats with clean, dry deck carpets look inviting, and carpets are an easy, inexpensive way to give an older boat a new look.

Interior Carpet

The best way to keep interior carpets clean is to use runners that are easy to remove and clean. Buying throw rugs or runners with a rubber backing at a variety or carpet store is a good solution, but a better solution is to have canvas runners cut to match the layout of your boat's interior and install snaps or hooks to attach them to the carpet and keep them in place. This type of runner will do a better job of keeping stains from touching any part of the carpet because the runners will have been measured to fit your interior's carpeted area and therefore will cover almost every inch of it. There won't be any sections that aren't protected, as in the case with two runners that don't match up perfectly. And the installed canvas carpet covers will stay in place better.

If you choose to install canvas carpet covers, have them treated with a stain guard before they are brought on board. Also, request that the sewn-in loops that will connect to the hooks in the cabin carpet are slightly elastic. Over time, these carpet runners shrink when cleaned and dried, and it can be very difficult to reattach them to the hooks in the cabin carpet.

To clean canvas carpet covers, simply remove them from the boat and wash and dry them at home or in a laundromat as you would the canvas covers used on the exterior of the boat. Use the warm-water setting on the washer and the low heat setting on the dryer. Or have a professional cleaning service clean and dry them for you.

If you don't use this type of interior carpet protection, the best way to keep your carpets clean is to remove stains as quickly as possible to keep them from setting in and to have your carpets professionally cleaned at the end of each boating season. You can use a store-bought carpet cleaner spray, but sometimes making your own from natural products, either on their own or used with a store-bought cleaner, will do a better job of removing stains and will certainly be less expensive. A commercial carpet cleaner in my area (D. A. Burns, in Seattle) provided me with the following list of cleaning solutions to use on specific carpet stains. For each stain listed, one or more of these solutions may be required, together with some white absorbent towels or rags, to remove most or all of the stain.

Cleaning Solutions (Ingredients or Products)

▶ **Detergent solution.** Carpet cleaner like Spot Off or Folex, or mix your own: 1 teaspoon clear, mild liquid dishwashing detergent and 1 cup lukewarm water.

▶ **Ammonia solution.** Mix 1 tablespoon household ammonia with ½ cup warm water. (Use less ammonia for wool carpet.)

▶ **Vinegar solution.** Mix ⅓ cup white household vinegar with ⅔ cup water.

▶ **Enzyme detergent.** Commercial enzyme detergent like Nature's Miracle.

▶ **Dry-cleaning solvent.** Commercial volatile dry spotter like Energine or Spot Off.

Recommended Procedures

1. Test the solution on a small, inconspicuous area, then tackle the stain by working from the outer edge towards the center; blot, don't rub.
2. The final spot-removal step is always to gently rinse the area with water, then soak up all the remaining moisture with absorbent towels.
3. When finished, place a half-inch pad of white absorbent paper towels over the affected area and weight it down with a flat, heavy object.
4. Change the absorbent pad until the spilled substance or residue is no longer visible on the pad.

Stain	Cleaning Solutions
Blood	Detergent, ammonia, enzyme
Chocolate	Detergent, ammonia, vinegar, enzyme
Coffee or tea	Detergent, vinegar, enzyme
Fats	Dry cleaning, detergent, vinegar
Fruit juice	Detergent, ammonia, vinegar, enzyme
Glue	Detergent, ammonia, vinegar
Gravy	Detergent, ammonia, vinegar, enzyme
Grease	Dry cleaning, detergent, ammonia, vinegar
Gum	Dry cleaning, detergent
Ice cream	Detergent, ammonia, vinegar
Lipstick	Dry cleaning, detergent, ammonia, vinegar
Milk	Detergent, ammonia, vinegar, enzyme
Nail polish	Dry cleaning, detergent, ammonia, vinegar
Oil or tar	Dry cleaning, detergent
Paint (oil base)	Dry cleaning, detergent, ammonia, vinegar
Paint (water base)	Detergent, ammonia, vinegar, dry cleaning
Shoe polish	Dry cleaning, detergent, ammonia, vinegar
Soft drinks	Detergent, ammonia, vinegar
Tomato sauce or ketchup	Detergent, ammonia, vinegar, enzyme

Urine	Detergent, ammonia, vinegar
Vomit	Enzyme, ammonia, vinegar
Wax	Dry cleaning, detergent, heat gun
Wine	Detergent, ammonia, vinegar

Vinyl Seats and Cushions

Vinyl seats and cushions are fairly easy to keep clean if you keep them dry. Vinyl is smooth and therefore easy to clean with a multipurpose spray cleaner, but because vinyl is technically a fabric, it can absorb water and, if not allowed to dry out, can foster the growth of mildew. Left untreated, the mildew is difficult to remove. If you don't plan on treating the mildew in your vinyl cushions, simply buy pink cushions to begin with and you won't even notice the mildew. That's because mildew that's been left on vinyl for a long time will eventually turn the vinyl pink. But more on this later.

Gear and Supplies

The following items will help remove stains and prevent stains or other elements (UV rays, salt water) from causing additional wear and tear.

- Mr. Clean Magic Eraser cleaning pads
- Mildew spray cleaner, such as Lysol or Tilex
- Multipurpose cleaner, such as Inflatable Boat Cleaner, Black Streak Remover, or Krazy Clean (all are available at boat supply stores)
- 303 Aerospace Protectant
- Microfiber rags

Removing Bird and Spider Stains

Bird droppings are acidic and high in nitrogen in the form of ammonia, a molecule formed from nitrogen and hydrogen. When the droppings dry out, the product produced is a salt—a chemical compound that forms when a base, in this case ammonia, reacts with an acid. Over time, the salt causes metal to rust and gelcoat or fabric to become etched or develop pinholes. This alone is an excellent reason to wax your boat so the bird droppings sit on top of the wax. Likewise, it's an excellent reason to clean the vinyl seating on your boat to keep the vinyl from breaking down over time.

If birds use your exterior vinyl seats for target practice and spiders use your interior vinyl seats as their own personal restroom (spider droppings look like small black dots), your vinyl probably needs to be restored to its white state, then heavily protected to prevent future stains. Once these stains have had a chance to "soak" into vinyl, they can be difficult to remove with just a spray cleaner and a rag.

You'll want to purchase two items for this task. The first is a Mr. Clean Magic Eraser pad (Extra Power), which you can buy at most grocery or variety stores. Buy the ones that are white, not blue and white, because it's the white side that you'll be using on the vinyl. The other product you'll need is either Inflatable Boat Cleaner or Black Streak Remover, available at boating supply stores. Once you have these items, along with rubber gloves and a microfiber rag, you are ready to begin.

Spray the cleaner (Inflatable Boat Cleaner or Black Streak Remover) over the vinyl, then take the magic pad and lightly wipe it over the areas you've sprayed. If there is a stain (ink, bird, or spider droppings, drink stains, et cetera), use a light amount of pressure over that particular area. This should remove all stains and "graying" from dirt and grime and make your vinyl white again.

Once you've used the magic pad to clean the vinyl, it's now time to protect it again since the magic pads contain a light abrasive agent and will have removed any protectant you originally had on them. Spray on the 303 Aerospace Protectant and wipe it in with a microfiber rag. Your white vinyl seats and cushions should

Vinyl with water stains

The Magic Eraser pad is excellent for cleaning vinyl.

shine again like new, and future stains will sit on top of the protectant and be easier to clean off rather than soaking into the vinyl fabric over time.

Removing Mildew

And now back to that pink vinyl. There are ways to prevent this from ever happening to your vinyl, and it all relates to keeping your exterior seat cushions dry. If they are removable, bring them inside the boat or your garage for dry storage through the wet months. If they are not removable, protect them with a canvas or plastic cover. Make sure there is a small amount of breathing space so air can get through or under the cover; otherwise, the cushions won't dry out if they get damp or moist from windy and rainy weather.

If there is mildew on your vinyl, whether it is black or green, spray one side of the cushion with mildew spray and use a soft hand brush or light scrub brush to work the mildew out of the vinyl "grain." The scrub brush is ideal for getting mildew out of rolled edges and seams. Either hose off or wipe off the mildew cleaner and let that surface dry. Turn the cushion over and spritz it with mildew cleaner spray as well. You can wipe it off with a rag or just let it soak in to prevent future mildew growth. When finished, let the cushions dry completely. Then use the 303 Aerospace Protectant to further protect the vinyl from UV rays and stains.

The best way to prevent stains on your vinyl seats and cushions is to protect the vinyl material. Conditioner won't soak in to vinyl the way it soaks in to leather. But you can keep vinyl from drying out or breaking down over time from constant contact with UV rays. A product called 303 Aerospace Protectant, available at boating supply stores, is similar to ArmorAll, used on car interiors, but is made for marine conditions and contains slightly stronger UV protectants. Spray the protectant over the vinyl, being sure to cover all sides and edges, and rub it in with a microfiber rag. This will make your vinyl seats shine, protect them from UV rays, and make them more stain resistant. Spray them with this product once a month to keep them in good condition.

Interior Fabrics

When shopping for interior fabrics such as curtains, bedding, towels, and throw rugs or carpet runners, make sure they are easy to attach and reconnect (curtains) and can be easily removed (duvet covers or carpet runners) so you can wash and dry them as needed.

Curtains can be vacuumed in between washes to remove dust. Duvet covers are better than comforters because they're easier to remove, wash, and dry. Throw rugs and carpet runners can easily be vacuumed or taken up and washed at home or by a rug cleaning service. If you don't use your boat during cold, wet, or winter months, you should remove as many of these interior fabrics as you can, wash and dry them, and store them in a dry place until spring.

Fabric seat cushion covers should be removed and run through a washer and dryer. If the covers aren't removable but the cushions aren't very large or thick, you can put the entire cushion in a washer and dryer. Otherwise, you can take them to a commercial fabric cleaner, who can also treat the cushions with a stain guard to prevent future stains from soaking in as easily.

If you have vinyl headboards or wall panels, take a multipurpose cleaner and a Mr. Clean magic pad, spray the stain with the cleaner, and lightly wipe the stain away with the magic pad.

CHAPTER 7

Natural Cleaning Products

As recreational boaters, we enjoy watching nature take place around us, whether we're simply sitting on our boat in its slip at the marina or cruising on fresh or salt water. I always enjoy watching blue herons stealthily hunt for fish or seals and otters stick their heads out of the water to see what's going on in our world.

I often wonder just how clean our waterways are for these creatures—the mammals, the water fowl, and the fish—and what we can do to prevent adding more pollution to their environment. This chapter covers:

▶ Defining "biodegradable"
▶ And the award for "best cleaner" goes to . . .
▶ Cleaning with baking soda, vinegar, and hydrogen peroxide
▶ Other useful household cleaners
▶ Handy quick guide to natural cleaning products

But the Boat Soap Says Biodegradable . . .

Most of the boat cleaning and washing products you'll find at boating supply stores are marked "biodegradable." This simply means that these products can be decomposed by biological agents in the water, such as bacteria. A biodegradable product like boat soap eventually "breaks down" in the water, as opposed to remaining in its current form, such as oil. However, biodegradable products can still kill or sicken waterfowl and fish. This is because most soaps and other cleaning agents contain phosphates.

Phosphates encourage plant growth by enabling plant leaves to make food. While small amounts of phosphates are good for the environment, large amounts are harmful. Phosphates biodegrade slowly and their effects are felt for a long time. Phosphates increase the acidity of the water and speed up the growth of algae, which blocks light and chokes water flow, making it difficult for other living organisms (plants and fish) to exist in that environment. In essence, phosphates slowly suffocate the creatures living in that area. Algae rob other plants of the nourishment they need to survive, and decaying plant material uses up the available oxygen in the water when these plants die.

When you purchase boat soap or any type of surfactant (a surface activating agent), make sure it contains little or no phosphates. Any boat soap or cleaner that does not contain phosphates will most likely tout that on the label, so it will be easy to find the phosphate-free cleaners among all the others. One type of soap that should never be used to wash your boat is liquid dish soap. Although many brands are biodegradable, they are high in phosphates, which is what produces all of the suds that we associate with a "hardworking" soap. The biodegradable or low-phosphate soaps that you'll find at boat supply stores will still do a good job of getting your boat clean while having less negative impact on local waterways. Liquid dish soap is also fairly drying and can strip wax over time.

And the Award for Best Cleaner Goes To . . .

Wax. The liquid and paste waxes available at boating supply stores aren't necessarily considered natural products (although brands like Zymol and waxes that are made mostly of carnauba are more natural), but wax is one of the best "cleaners" you can use on your boat for the sole reason that it stays on the boat! It doesn't get washed or rinsed off only to end up in the water, yet it's a very versatile cleaner. (Yes, wax dust ends up in the air when you buff it off the boat, but those small particles are spread over a greater area and become more "diluted" than the amount of boat soap that is washed into the water.)

Some good uses for wax as a cleaner include:

▶ Cleaning water stains from gelcoat
▶ Polishing and protecting chrome rails
▶ Removing rust from stainless and other metals
▶ Removing shoe scuff marks from gelcoat
▶ Removing stains left on gelcoat from bird and spider droppings
▶ Removing water spots from exterior windows
▶ Removing marks made by lines rubbing across gelcoat

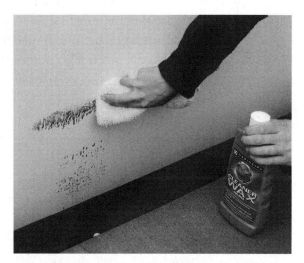

Use cleaner wax to remove scuff marks and other marks in gelcoat.

Look for a cleaner wax (liquid as opposed to paste, such as Meguiar's Cleaner Wax or SeaPower) because it contains a light-grade rubbing compound and will remove more types of marks and stains than a soft wax that contains no rubbing compound.

If It's Good for Cookies . . .

A few ingredients in your kitchen or galley also work well as cleaning products or as a component of natural cleaning products. These ingredients are much less expensive than chemical cleaners, are healthier for your respiratory system and the environment, and help save room in boat storage compartments. Keep one large box of baking soda and a bottle of vinegar in a cupboard instead of several spray bottles of chemical cleaners.

Baking Soda

Baking soda is one of the most widely used natural cleaning products available. Baking soda (or bicarbonate of soda, as it is also known) is a naturally occurring material, present in most organic life forms. It can be "made" from sodium carbonate, or soda ash. When soda ash is dissolved in a carbon-dioxide-rich solution, sodium bicarbonate (baking soda) precipitates out. It's versatile and inexpensive, has no toxic scent or ingredients, can be used as a dry powder or liquid paste, and can be found at all grocery and household variety stores. To make a paste from baking soda, simply mix it with water until you have the desired thickness for its purpose. Here are a few ways to use baking soda on your boat:

- ▶ Scrub dirt out of the nonskid "pockets"
- ▶ Soak up oil or grease stains on the nonskid and teak decks (powder form)
- ▶ Polish stainless steel
- ▶ Remove rust on metal deck hardware
- ▶ Clean stains on vinyl (paste form)
- ▶ Freshen fridges, freezers, cupboards, and heads (powder form)
- ▶ Remove tarnish from silver that has been in contact with aluminum foil (powder dissolved in warm water)
- ▶ Put out small fires (powder form)

A more natural way to clean nonskid

Don't use baking soda, either in powder or paste form, to remove stains from smooth gelcoat. Baking soda acts as a light abrasive and it will remove not only the stain but the wax on your gelcoat. If you do use baking soda to remove a stain on smooth gelcoat, follow it up with wax in that area. (Or just use cleaner wax to remove the stain and you won't have to follow up with anything.) Also, do not use baking soda to clean aluminum objects; it attacks the thin nonreactive protective oxide layer of this otherwise very reactive metal.

Vinegar

White household vinegar is a weak form of acetic acid that forms through the fermentation of sugars or starches. It is completely edible and cannot harm your stomach. And luckily for us, it can be used to clean many things. Although it has a pungent odor, vinegar has so many uses that you should have at least a few bottles of it on your boat at all times. Try some of these tips with vinegar and a few other natural household ingredients:

▶ For spills on carpet, use a sponge or cloth to soak up as much liquid as possible. Then spray the area with a mixture of half vinegar, half water. Let stand for about two minutes, then blot with a towel or sponge. Repeat as needed. For more persistent stains, use a mixture of 1 teaspoon vinegar, 1 teaspoon liquid dish soap, and 1 cup warm water. Proceed as suggested above. Then dry the spot with a hair dryer set on low.

▶ To clean windows, spray with half vinegar, half water. Wipe clean with newspapers or a cloth.

▶ To clean silver, pewter, copper, or brass, dissolve 1 teaspoon salt in 1 cup vinegar. Add flour to make a paste (you should have ¼ cup or more). Apply the paste to the metal item, and let stand for at least 15 minutes. Rinse with warm water and polish with a soft cloth.

▶ To clean wood paneling, use a mixture of 1/2 cup olive oil, 1/2 cup vinegar, and 2 cups warm water. Apply to paneling with a soft cloth. Dry with a clean cloth.

▶ To remove corrosion or chemical buildup from showerheads, soak in vinegar overnight.

▶ Remove stains from a toilet bowl by spraying with vinegar. To remove calcium scale inside marine toilets and discharge hoses, which can cause the toilet to get progressively harder to flush and eventually lead to total blockage, pour 1 pint (2 cups) white vinegar into the bowl once a month and pump it slowly (a single stroke every four to five minutes) through the toilet. The mildly acidic vinegar dissolves fresh scale deposits.

▶ To remove soap buildup from faucets, clean with a mixture of one part salt to four parts vinegar.

▶ Spray shower walls and shower curtains with mixture of vinegar and water to help prevent mildew.

▶ To clean wooden cutting boards, wipe with vinegar.

▶ Polish tarnished brass with 1 tablespoon each flour, salt, and vinegar. Apply the paste with a clean, damp rag, and rub off the tarnish. Wipe off the residue with a dry rag.

▶ Remove hard water stains by spraying them with vinegar (simply pour some into a spray bottle) and rinse with fresh water.

Cleaning with Peroxide

Hydrogen peroxide is odorless and colorless, but not tasteless. Cleaning with hydrogen peroxide—also referred to as H_2O_2—is one of the easiest ways to make sure that you provide a safer, cleaner space, with lower bacteria levels, but without the risk of the toxicity that is sometimes associated with commercial chemical spray cleaners.

▶ Clean appliances, countertops, and the inside of the refrigerator with hydrogen peroxide. It not only cleans and shines everything, it kills germs. While you're at it, pour a drop of peroxide right onto your cutting board to destroy bacteria, like salmonella.

▶ Make your dishes sparkle and disinfect the dishwasher at the same time. Pour a capful of peroxide in the pre-wash compartment, fill the compartment with dishwashing detergent, and run the cycle. While that's cleaning, give your plants a lift by adding 1 tablespoon peroxide to their water.

▶ Forget harsh chemicals like bleach to brighten your whites. Add a capful (no more) of peroxide to your washer along with your soap. Don't overdo it, though, because peroxide is acidic and could harm delicate fabric.

▶ Keep a spray bottle of peroxide in the bathroom. Mix a solution of 50 percent peroxide to 50 percent water. Spray down the shower when you're finished bathing to prevent mold and mildew from forming.

▶ Pour 1 cup hydrogen peroxide in the toilet and let it sit overnight. Scrub the toilet in the morning, and the bowl will be super clean.

▶ Remove bloodstains from clothing, upholstery, and carpet with peroxide. Pour a dab directly on the spot and let it soak for one minute. Promptly rinse with warm water and blot dry with a clean cloth. Repeat as necessary. The peroxide works as an oxidizer to lift stains.

Other Useful Household Cleaners

If you need a light abrasive cleaner or paste cleaner to use on specific areas of the boat, mix baking soda, salt, sugar, or cornstarch with water. Use a sliced lemon dipped in salt to clean brass, then wipe it off with a clean, dry rag. Remove new rust stains on fiberglass with a mixture of cola and salt, then rinse with clean water.

Remember, ammonia can etch aluminum and make Plexiglas or Lexan look cloudy. When using it, avoid letting it touch those materials, and rinse the area where you're working with fresh water often.

Alternatives to Mildew-Cleaning Spray

These products can contain bleach; sodium hypochlorite, a bleaching and disinfecting agent that is corrosive and can burn the skin and eyes; and formaldehyde, a highly toxic chemical and known carcinogen. For mold and mildew removal, mix 2 teaspoons tea tree oil (available at health food stores) in 2 cups water and keep in a spray bottle. Spray onto mold or mildew. Don't rinse. The strong smell fades in a couple of days. This solution also removes musty odors from fabrics such as cushions and curtains. Spray the fabric thoroughly so that it's wet, then let it air-dry for a few days until the fragrance of the tea tree oil subsides. For mold and mildew on non-porous washable surfaces, try vinegar or a solution of borax and water.

If You Need Something Stronger than Baking Ingredients . . .

If you have a stain that won't go away after trying the more natural products, use a stronger chemical cleaning product (like what you would buy in the cleaning aisle of a supermarket). But instead of hosing the product off the boat, take an absorbent rag and wipe it off or soak it up. Examples of "stronger" cleaning products are Lysol Mildew Remover, Black Streak Remover, adhesive remover, and cleaners that contain mostly chemicals, acids, or bleach. Read the back of the bottle to see what the product contains. Remember, just because it says "biodegradable" doesn't mean it is good for waterways. It can still kill wildlife and plant life.

Wiping away a chemical cleaner prevents it from contaminating our waterways.

Handy Quick Guide to Natural Cleaning Products

Stain or Use	Solution—Main Ingredient
Blood and other proteins	Peroxide
Boat soap	Vinegar
Brass	Vinegar and salt
Carpet stains	Vinegar
Clothes—brighten in wash	Peroxide
Copper	Vinegar and salt
Deodorizer	Baking soda
Dishes, dishwasher	Peroxide
Disinfectant	Peroxide
Germ killer	Peroxide
Grease stains	Baking soda
Hard-water stains	Vinegar
Metal corrosion	Vinegar
Mildew prevention	Vinegar or peroxide
Pewter	Vinegar and salt
Room odors	Vinegar
Rust on metal	Cleaner wax or baking soda
Scuff marks on gelcoat	Cleaner wax
Silver	Vinegar and salt
Soap buildup	Vinegar
Tarnish on silver	Baking soda
Toilet bowl stains	Vinegar
Water stains, streaks, and spots	Cleaner wax
Windows (glass only)	Vinegar
Wine stains	Peroxide
Wood cutting board	Vinegar or peroxide
Wood paneling	Vinegar

CHAPTER **8**

Cleaning While Cruising

Summer has arrived and you're taking your family on a three-week cruise up and down the coast or maybe to some islands nearby. You've stocked the boat with everyone's favorite food and beverages, fun movies to watch in the evenings, and the new electronics you bought yourself last Christmas, finally having a chance to use them all. But did you remember to pack a boat cleaning kit with the items you'll need along the way to keep your boat clean and protected from the elements? It takes just a few minutes while you're under way or once you've docked to keep your boat clean in all the right places so it doesn't become too big a chore once you're back at your home slip.

This chapter discusses:

▶ The importance of cleaning while cruising
▶ Exterior cleaning—gear, supplies, and techniques
▶ Interior cleaning—gear, supplies, and techniques

The Importance of Cleaning While Cruising

When you're out cruising on salt water, your boat is getting hit with all of the elements that can be thrown at it, and often all at once. Water, salt, UV rays, dirt particles in the air, pollution (in the form of dirty or acid rain), bird droppings, and maybe even fish blood (if you're so lucky). Consider that if you're on a two- to three-week cruise, your boat will be exposed to these elements every day and, if they're not properly removed, they will wreak havoc on your gelcoat and windows to the point that the gelcoat will start looking faded and window cleaner will no longer get your windows clean and free of water spots.

Consider also that as you and your family spend more time on your boat, every time you brush up against the side of the house structure or roll up a plastic window panel, you're causing the dirt and salt particles to lightly scratch those areas. Salt spray does the most damage to finishes and materials on a boat. Imagine that you've just pulled into port and secured your boat in its slip. There is a light film of salt spray all over your boat—on the hull, the decks and abovedeck structures and the windows, and even in the nonskid. The sun's rays shining through each droplet of salt as if it were a small mirror will cause the salt to burn or etch whatever it's sitting on. You'll see the damage of salt spray on darker-colored materials quite easily—for example, on a dark-colored hull or tinted windows. The damage done by salt spray still occurs on light-colored materials or clear windows, and although it won't be as obvious, it still needs to be removed.

If you've been cruising on fresh water, you won't have to worry about salt spray on your boat, but the dirt particles in the air and other types of stains and marks will still affect the cosmetic appearance and protective nature of the gelcoat. Once you've arrived in your slip, you'll probably want to head out and go sightseeing or join up with your friends, but take a few minutes to clean your boat so that none of the elements that landed on it do any actual damage. You'll have less of a headache later and hopefully be able to prevent salt spray or water spots from becoming permanent additions to your glass and plastic windows.

Exterior Cleaning

You probably already have most of what you'll need to clean your boat stored in a lazarette. The most obvious items are a hose, nozzle, boat soap, and a soft deck brush. Make sure you also have the following:

- ▶ Large pack of microfiber rags
- ▶ Squeegee, preferably a California Water Blade
- ▶ Mr. Clean magic pads
- ▶ Cleaner wax like Meguiar's or SeaPower

- ▸ Soft hand brush and small scrub brush
- ▸ Plastic window cleaner like Mer-maids Plastic Cleaner or Meguiar's #17 Mirror Glaze Plastic Cleaner

The best arsenal to have on a trip

You cannot just hose down your boat and call it good, unfortunately. Salt cannot be hosed off because all you've done is simply hosed off the salt crystal. There will still be salt residue on your gelcoat or windows, and the only way to remove that is to wash it off with soap and a soft brush. If your boat has been recently waxed or still has a good coat of wax on it, the salt will be easier to wash off, and this chore will go much faster because it will take only one pass with the soft deck brush and some soap and water to remove it.

> *Tip:* The best squeegee I've found for quickly and easily drying a whole boat is the California Water Blade. Buy the larger rectangular one, not angled on the edges, because it's more flexible and works better on larger surfaces.

Keep all of your washing gear together where it is quickly and easily accessible so that once you've docked, you can grab it from one place and get to work. If you have a mate to help you, one of you can operate the hose and one can work the deck brush. Spray the boat thoroughly to remove most of the salt crystals, bird droppings, and sand or dirt that has been tracked on the boat, then follow up with the soft deck brush and soapy water. Work from the top down so everything drains down and off.

If you've tracked sand on the boat, spend a few extra minutes hosing it off the boat (as well as hosing off the two- and four-legged creatures that brought it on the boat). Sand is an abrasive that can scratch gelcoat. It can also slowly clog drains, so spray the hose in all of your drains to make sure they're not clogged.

When you are finished washing the boat, squeegee as many areas as you can to prevent any water spotting, especially if the boat is sitting in direct sunlight. Squeegee the windows as well, because that will help you prepare for the next step.

If you've been cruising on salt water, spend the majority of your time getting the windows (whether glass, Lexan, or plastic) completely clean. You'll want to make sure you've removed all the salt crystals from them so they don't leave permanent spots. Even if you've washed down the windows with soap and water when you washed the boat, they may still have a salt residue. Take a good look at them after rinsing them several times to make sure they are salt-free.

If they're not, grab some plastic window cleaner (even for the glass windows) and several clean, dry microfiber rags. Spray the plastic window cleaner generously on each window, then wipe it down with a microfiber rag. On your second pass, spray the window again but with only a few light squirts of window cleaner. Take another microfiber rag (not the one you just used because it now has salt residue on it and will only put the salt back on the window you're trying to clean) and wipe the window again. Now look at the window from all angles. Your dock neighbors will think you're either obsessed or blind, but this is the only way to completely remove all of the salt residue from the windows. If left on, the residue will cause permanent spotting on the windows, which will no longer come off with just a spray cleaner and rag.

Naturally, if you've been cruising with friends or family for long periods of time, there are bound to be stains and marks on the gelcoat and nonskid. The best way to quickly clean nonskid is to wipe it with a dampened Mr. Clean Magic pad. For grease stains, you can spritz them with a degreaser cleaner spray, wipe the magic pad over that section, then wipe it with a rag. To remove scuff marks or other stains and marks from smooth gelcoat, use a microfiber rag to apply a small amount of cleaner wax to the area. Let it dry to a haze and then wipe off. Cleaner wax is an excellent "cleaner" to use all over your boat because it quickly and easily removes stains or marks on most surfaces, including plastics, glass, and stainless steel and other metals.

Use a Magic Eraser pad to remove black marks from nonskid.

Interior Cleaning

The four main items you should have on hand for quick interior cleaning are:

- ▶ Vacuum that is easy to store and quick and easy to use
- ▶ Microfiber rags
- ▶ Multipurpose spray cleaner
- ▶ Tub of disinfecting wipes like Clorox Disinfecting Wipes
- ▶ Carpet spot remover like Folex

Once a day, vacuum all surfaces to remove crumbs on cushions or counters, floor dirt, hair in the shower or around the toilet, and dog hair. Keeping on top of vacuuming crumbs and dirt as you go along will make a huge difference in how long it takes to do a final cleaning once you're back from your cruise. And daily vacuuming should keep you from swimming in dog hair. If you have berber or short-pile carpets and the vacuum doesn't remove most of the dog hair, try lifting it with a wide strip of tape (painter's tape or packing tape). This is one of the best ways to thoroughly remove dog hair from carpet. Or . . . brown dog? Buy brown runners.

It's best to choose a multipurpose spray cleaner that can be used on all surfaces, like mirrors, granite, veneer, stainless, or plastic. I prefer SprayWay because I've never found it to streak or leave a haze on any surface. You can find this product in the window cleaning section of grocery or variety stores. Keeping a product like this on board allows you to quickly spray and wipe any surface without having to store several different cleaning products or carry around several products as you go about the boat wiping down surfaces.

Disinfecting wipes are useful for cleaning the toilet and surrounding areas, as well as kitchen counters and handles that are often touched by everyone. They're a good way to keep heavily used areas clean and germ-free.

Remove stains on carpets as quickly as you can with a carpet spot remover and a small scrub brush or even an old toothbrush. This will keep the stains from permanently setting in. After cleaning these spots, put down an old washcloth or paper towels to soak up any excess cleaner so the spots dry faster and people or pets don't walk on them while they're drying.

In fact, you may want to purchase carpet runners just for the trip you're planning to take. These will greatly improve the chances that you won't come back with badly stained carpeting that requires the services of a professional carpet cleaner.

When your your trip is over, the runners can easily be cleaned and stored for your next cruise.

Spot cleaning while cruising is the best way to keep on top of stains, marks, and spots that, if left alone, could create a lot more work for you when you return from your cruise. Water spots that are left to sit on windows eventually etch into the glass or plastic and will be much more difficult to remove in the future, if you're able to remove them at all. If you're cruising with friends and family, assign everyone on board a task for them to take care of. Make sure each activity above gets done once each day. Unfortunately, until someone comes up with microfiber dog slippers and tail swishers, your four-legged skipper, who probably makes the biggest mess of all, won't be able to join in and ease your cleaning load.

CHAPTER **9**

Hiring a Detailer

Washing, waxing, and detailing your boat can be a big job, whether your boat is 30 feet or 60 feet long. Aside from taking a lot of time to keep your boat in good condition, it also takes energy, flexibility, balance, skill, and physical exertion. If you don't have the time and/or physical ability to do it all yourself, consider hiring a boat cleaner/detailer to do the work for you, especially if it means that the work won't get done otherwise.

Taking care of light maintenance issues now, no matter who does the work, can save a lot of headaches later. If, every time you set foot on your boat, washing or cleaning it takes away from the time you actually spend using and enjoying your boat, hiring a detailer can be liberating. Imagine being able to dock your boat on a Sunday evening after a weekend of cruising and head straight home instead of spending an hour or two washing down the boat and vacuuming the potato chip crumbs off the carpet. When you've had too much wine, and "red, right, return" has tapped out your mental abilities, it's a lot easier to dial your detailer than do the cleaning yourself.

Here are some tips on how to find and hire a good detailer and what you can expect them to do. This chapter includes information on:

- ▶ Where to find a detailer and what to look for
- ▶ Cost of hiring a detailer
- ▶ Working with a detailer
- ▶ What to do if the detailer missed something

Where to Find a Detailer and What to Look For

You'll recognize good detailers when you see them, bundled up in their winter rain gear, washing boats in 35-degree weather while dealing with frozen hoses and runny noses. These are not the fair-weathered detailers who swoop in from June to September to see what work they can drum up for the summer, but rather the year-round, dedicated detailers who have most likely been at it for a long time and are still at it (even in winter) because they love their work.

Frozen hoses and runny noses—good detailers work year-round.

The best way to find a good detailer is to ask around. Who does your dock neighbor use? Who stops in at the boat supply store on a regular basis to buy more products? Who do the marinas recommend? Who does the brokerage you bought your boat from use? Here are a few things that any good detailer will have, use, or do.

- ▶ They will have insurance and a business license.
- ▶ They will use products made for gelcoat and boats rather than household or auto products (except where the latter are appropriate).
- ▶ They will not use harsh chemicals or cleaners on their first pass, but will use them only as a last resort and will be careful about disposing of them.
- ▶ They will have references you can check.
- ▶ They will call you if the work will cost more or take longer than the quote or schedule they originally gave you.
- ▶ They have experience working on different types of boats, coatings, and finishes and are capable of dealing with problem areas (specific types of stains, scratches, et cetera).

If you're still unsure about who to use, call around. You can find detailers listed in The Boaters Yellow Pages (www.boatersyellowpages.com) and on Yachtworld (www.yachtworld.com). You can also find business cards posted at your yacht club, marina, or favorite boat supply store. Decide to call three to five detailers and ask each of them the same questions, including what is their experience, what products do they use, what is their process for washing or waxing a boat, and what are their rates. It will be easy for you to decide who to choose because, out of five calls, most likely only one or two will call you back!

The Cost of Hiring a Detailer

As for rates and prices, there are really no set prices in the detailing industry. You can negotiate, but don't think this is a service you can get at a rock-bottom rate. A good detailer will spend a lot of time and physical exertion and use quality products on your boat. These are worth paying for if you can't or don't want to do the work yourself.

Some detailers charge by the hour and some charge by the foot. If they charge by the foot, you'll know up front exactly what the total cost will be. If they charge by the hour, at least ask them to give you an estimate of how long they think the job will take and let you know ahead of time if they expect to exceed that time. If they do exceed the original number of hours, ask them to give you an updated estimate and explain why it's taking longer. They may have run into a few problem areas you should know about or they may have underestimated the job when they first gave you the quote.

If they severely underestimated the job, you might question them as to why they didn't fully realize the scope of the project in the beginning. For example, if you hired a detailer to wax and buff your heavily oxidized boat and they gave you a "sounds too good to be true" quote, they either low-balled the quote to beat out any other bids or they may not have enough experience to know that heavy oxidation often requires a two-step process, which takes longer, uses more product, and requires a skilled hand at buffing.

In trying to negotiate a fair rate or a price that fits your budget, consider two things: (1) Try to do some of the work yourself and (2) decide what's most important to you. For example, you might be able to save a few dollars if you wash the boat yourself so that the detailer has to only wax and buff it. Or, if you feel you have the time and energy to wax and buff the decks and abovedeck structures (usually the easier part of the boat to reach and work on), hire them to wax and buff only the hull. Regarding what is most important to you, is your goal a well-protected boat or a cosmetically perfect finish? In the case of having your boat waxed, if you're mostly concerned with simply protecting the gelcoat with a good layer of wax, a one-step wax process is all you need. If you are determined to bring back the showroom shine and the gelcoat is heavily oxidized, prepare to pay for a two-step wax process, which is often double the rate of a one-step process.

Finally, ask the detailer if there are any additional charges in their rate. Depending on your state, some detailers must charge sales tax because their services are considered "retail sales." However, some might also charge for supplies, special equipment, gear specifically used for your boat, mileage or other transportation, and labor fees. Have them itemize and explain any additional charges before they start the work.

Working with a Detailer

Communication is key! The first thing you should do when you meet with your new detailer is communicate to them exactly what you want them to do and what your expectations are.

For example, if you hire a detailer to wash your boat, are you expecting them to clean out the hatches, polish the chrome, wipe down the flybridge, and clean the canvas covers, or simply wash the gelcoat and nonskid? Does washing the boat include the dinghy? The detailer might consider "washing a boat" as washing the structure and nonskid of the boat, whereas you might consider that service to include everything on the outside of the boat. Tell the detailer exactly what you expect to be included with the service so there are no surprises for either of you, both in the quality of the work and the final bill.

A solid customer-detailer relationship is important.

Defining terminology is also important. When I'm describing my services to a new customer, I divide the general term of "boat cleaning" into four categories. This way, they'll know exactly what my services include and I'll know exactly what they're expecting. For example:

- ▶ Washing—the boat's structure, nonskid, and flybridge or helm area
- ▶ Detailing—cleaning or washing the Isenglass, polishing chrome rails, cleaning and brightening vinyl, cleaning out hatches, and cleaning canvas
- ▶ Waxing—waxing and buffing the boat by hand or with a power buffer, using rubbing compound if needed
- ▶ Interior cleaning—inside the boat

Here are few more tips about working with a detailer.

- ▶ Be realistic about what a detailer can and can't do for you. Heavily oxidized boat? Hire a detailer. Repair hairline cracks? No amount of wax or rubbing compound will buff these away. You'll need to hire a fiberglass repair service.
- ▶ Don't expect a 25-year-old boat or a boat that hasn't been washed or waxed in a long time (a couple of years or more) to look brand new again with a simple one-time wash and wax. It can certainly look good again, but it may require a few wax jobs to really bring out the gloss of the gelcoat, and it will definitely need to be put on a regular maintenance program.
- ▶ If you're uncertain about the products a detailer is using, request that they use specific products or provide them with the products you want them to use.
- ▶ Ask the detailer if they work alone or have a crew. If they have a crew that does most of the work, ask the detailer how often they check on their crew during the cleaning process. As I've always said, a worker won't care as much about the job as the business owner has to. Make sure the company owner or manager is on the job at some point for quality-control purposes.

What to Do If the Detailer Missed Something

If your detailer missed something the first time around, simply ask if they would come back to take care of that area. Most detailers are looking for specific problem areas or stains when cleaning a boat for the first time, as well as simply getting to know your boat and all of its nooks and crannies. If you see an area or a stain they missed, they didn't necessarily do a bad job; more possibly they overlooked it because they were focused on other details. Work with them so they gain a better understanding of your requirements and expectations, and over time you'll have a detailer you can count on who knows your boat inside and out, as well as your expectations.

If you ask the detailer to go back and work on an area you thought they missed, but they either refuse or tell you they'll have to charge you extra for cleaning a certain area twice, go back to that area with them and have them show you how they cleaned it originally. If they really did miss that spot and they clean the area while you're looking on, it will instantly look cleaner and it will be obvious if they missed it the first time around even if they said they didn't. If they clean it in front of you and the stain or dirt doesn't go away, removing the stain might require a stronger cleaner (for example, wax rather than soap). If you hired someone to wash your boat and there are many marks or stains that didn't come off with the wash, it's not the boat washer's fault unless you also asked that person to use wax to remove the marks when they were done washing the boat.

A Quick Note About the Crew

Boat detailers that come highly recommended are very busy people and often have a crew who do most of the work for them. If you've met the owner of the detailing company, most likely they will have looked and acted professionally. That may not be the case for their crew, but don't judge a book by its cover until you've seen their

A good detailer learns your boat and knows what it needs and when.

work. I try to hire people who actually want to do this sort of work (boat washing and waxing) as opposed to someone who just needs a job to earn a quick buck. But consider that very few people actually choose boat washing and waxing as their lifelong career. Trust me—it's not why they went to college! I know that I may get a good six to eighteen months out of each detailer I hire, either because after that amount of time they'll be ready to move on to a different job (maybe they finished college and are now ready to seek a job in their new field) or the work has become too physically laborious for them and, due to an injury or not wanting to deal with physical labor or harsh weather anymore, they decide to move on.

However, the owner of a good boat detailing company is in this business because they enjoy the work and they enjoy running their own business. They realize the importance of repeat customers and will try to do whatever it takes, within reason, to win your business. Give them time to get to know you and your boat. If things are still getting missed, it might be time to try another detailing service. Tell each detailer you'll give them a couple of chances before you move on to another company. Remember, boat detailers are only human and have to put up with harsh weather, physical labor, and dirty boats. Even detailers have their days!

CHAPTER **10**

A Year-Round Plan

I find checklists helpful because you can use them to follow a plan and know that you're not forgetting anything. This chapter offers some helpful checklists you can put into place every spring, summer, fall, and winter to prepare your boat for boating and maintain it on a regular basis.

Spring Checklist

One of the best things you can do in winter to prevent small things from becoming major issues by spring is to simply check on your boat at least once a month when you're not actively using it. If you use a boat washing service on a regular basis, ask them to keep an eye out for leaky windows or clogged drains or anything else that could become a larger problem if not easily dealt with during the off months. I provide regular washes for several boat owners in the Seattle area and, because I'm the one checking on their boat several times a month, I'm also the one checking lines before and after a windstorm, raking fallen leaves before they stain the gelcoat brown and purple, and alerting the owners of any leaks or other issues that need attention. Checking on your boat during the off months can make a big difference once it's time to tackle your pre–boating season check-

Spring cleaning is a good time to let your boat air out.

list. Assuming you achieved everything on the winter checklist (which we get to in a minute), your spring checklist should include the following activities:

- **Air out the inside.** Plan to spend a few hours on your boat one dry or sunny day. Open all doors and windows to let in fresh air. Turn on a small fan to help move the air around.

- **Freshen fabrics.** While you're airing out the boat, take all fabrics, such as bedding, cushions, and towels, that you left on the boat over the winter and hang them outside to freshen up. Put them back on the boat only if they're clean and dry and don't smell musty. If they do smell musty, bring them home and wash them.

- *Wax your boat!* Yes, I am yelling at you. I am a big proponent of waxing a boat because it's the best way to protect the gelcoat, help it stand up to weather and other elements you can't control, and make it easier to wash and keep clean. And wax keeps oxidation at bay, provided you wax your boat on a regular basis—at least once every nine to twelve months. It's the most eco-friendly cleaner there is because it's the only cleaner that stays on the surface as opposed to getting hosed off into the water. And fresh wax with a beautiful gloss increases a boat's resale value, regardless of its age.

- **Critters.** Take a quick look around your boat, especially in the exhaust openings and under the dinghy cover, to make sure no critters have made your boat their home over the winter. Muskrats love to crawl into the exhaust openings and burrow in, as well as use that entrance to your boat to get into other areas and chew their way around. This doesn't bode well for any tubes, pipes, or wires they come in contact with. I have found a raccoon family making a home in the enclosed flybridge and a bird family making a home under a dinghy cover on customers' boats. These present huge, stinky messes to clean up!

- **Mildew.** Ahh, mildew—the one constant for all boaters. When you get down to your boat in spring, you will see small black dots of mildew in the nonskid and areas of green mildew on the canvas, the rail, and possibly even the windowsills if you live in a wet climate. Spritz those areas with a mildew spray cleaner and work it in with a soft hand brush. Then wipe it off with a rag or spray it off with a hose.

- **Look for areas that may need repair.** Note potential problem areas—for example, if your boat was tied up in such a way that the swim platform bumped the edge of the dock, rubbing the gelcoat off that area. Or if a windstorm caused a piece of debris to nick the gelcoat. Now is the time to get those things repaired so they don't become larger problems later.

Spring is when most boaters are getting prepared for the boating season. So be aware that if you need to hire a maintenance business or contractor to service your boat, you should contact them in January so you can get on their schedule before they are booked through August. By the middle of February, my customer waxing schedule is booked well into May or June, so a customer calling in March hoping to get their boat waxed the following week is in for a big surprise when I tell them that our next opening is in June.

Summer and Early Fall Checklist

This is the time of year when you should be thoroughly enjoying your boat, whether you're sitting on it in its slip with an ice cold drink or cruising offshore with your friends and family. If you have prepared your boat in spring, it won't take much to keep it clean and looking good with these easy detailing tasks.

▶ **Schedule a wash program.** If your boat is in an uncovered slip or on saltwater or you use it often in the warmer months, put it on a recurring program where it is washed every two to three weeks. If it's in a covered slip, you can wash it every three to six weeks depending on how many spiders have chosen to live in the rafters above your boat. If you aren't able to wash your boat this often, consider hiring a boat detailing service to do it for you. They will put your boat on their recurring wash list and you won't have to worry about coming down to a very dirty boat.

▶ **Turn your boat.** Every now and then, dock your boat the other way when you come back from a trip. Then the side that is normally in the shade will get some sun, or vice versa, which can help prevent one side from becoming more faded or having more mildew growth than the other. Also, it's hard to wash the side of the hull that's away from the dock, and this will give you a chance to get that side fully clean again.

▶ **Touch-up cleaning goes a long way.** If your boat was waxed in spring, all you'll need to do during the more active boating months is use a little cleaner wax (such as Meguiar's Cleaner Wax or SeaPower) to remove bird dropping stains, scuff marks from shoes, and marks left from a power cord, fender, or line rubbing against the gelcoat.

▶ **Clean and polish plastic windows.** After each outing, use a product such as Mer-maids Plastic Cleaner or Plexus Plastic Polish to clean the plastic windows. Spray on and wipe off with a clean, dry microfiber rag.

▶ **Protect vinyl seats.** Vinyl seat cushions and seats can become dry and brittle, and crack over time if not cleaned and protected from UV rays. Use Simple Green or Black Streak Remover spray and a Mr. Clean magic pad to clean them and bring them back to white or their original color. These products remove dirt and any discoloration. Then spray with 303 Aerospace Protectant and wipe in with a microfiber rag. This protects them from UV rays and prevents them from drying out or cracking.

After cleaning vinyl seats, protect them with a UV protectant.

Winter Checklist

Now that Labor Day has passed and the hours of warm temperatures and daylight are fewer, it's time for you fair-weather boaters to start thinking about tucking your boat in for a long winter's nap if you live in a cooler climate. Here's a list of things you'll want to do or check before putting your boat away for the winter.

Interior Checklist

▶ **Clean and store all fabrics.** Remove any fabrics (curtains, bedspreads, blankets, towels, et cetera) from the boat, take them to the dry cleaners or wash them at home, and store them in your home or a dry storage unit. The less fabric and bedding on the boat, the fewer places mildew and moths can find to hide.

▶ **Clean the cushions.** Take any removable cushions to a dry cleaner to have them professionally cleaned and treated for soils and odors. These can go back on the boat, but prop them up so air can circulate around them. You never know when moisture might seep into your boat, and if cushions are upright rather than flat on the benches, there are fewer surfaces that can be contaminated by mildew.

▶ **Freshen cabinets.** Leave any storage cabinets and cupboards slightly ajar to air them out. I have found the storage compartments on some boats so airtight that if a small amount of moisture gets into them, they become a breeding ground for mold and mildew since no oxygen can get into the compartment to combat it.

▶ **Clean out the fridge and food cupboards.** Take food and beverage items off the boat to store at home or throw away. You really don't need to keep those seventeen half-eaten bags of potato chips for next year, so discard them now and start your collection all over again in spring. Clean out the fridge completely. Yes, even the ketchup! Take it all home or throw it out. I have never come across any food item or condiment that has improved with age in a boat fridge. Most condiments mysteriously drip, and most pop cans eventually explode. Get them all off your boat, clean the fridge, and wipe it completely dry. Place a box of baking soda in both the fridge and freezer. You might even want to turn off the fridge and leave it slightly ajar so it doesn't grow mildew over the winter.

▶ **Consider the unmentionable.** The more things you can take off your boat, the better. And I say this not just with mildew in mind. Consider what you might lose if a natural disaster were to occur, whether it be a storm, a fire, or the roof of your covered slip collapsing. If something were to happen to your boat, would you know what was on it so you could replace it? Remove anything that's priceless or expensive and make a checklist of everything that's left with an estimate of what it might be worth. If certain items must remain on the boat (electronics, audio and video equipment, et cetera), write down their serial numbers so you can give them to the insurance company. Additionally, make sure you know who your insurance company contact is and have their number in a handy place. It's no fun having to consider these things, but it's extremely helpful to have the information handy if anything does happen.

▶ **Condition the air inside.** Boats that are rained on all winter can smell musty or feel damp inside over time, especially older boats, wooden boats, and sailboats that don't have a fully sealed entry hatch where water can leak in. If you can safely put a space heater in the main salon where it's far enough from any fabrics or cords, this will be your best bet in keeping your boat at a warm enough air temperature to keep things dry. Of course, your goal is to condition the air so it doesn't cause humid conditions or dampness. A small portable air conditioner or dehumidifier will take the moisture out of the air and help prevent any moisture from "setting in" to the fabrics and wood grain of the boat interior. An ionizer helps, as well. If you are using a space heater, also set up a small fan to better circulate the air. Once a musty smell has set in to cushions, carpets, or any other fabric, it can be difficult to eliminate.

▶ **Mow the grass in the windowsills.** If you have any window leaks, now is the time to get the leaks fixed or the gaps filled. This is also a good time to make sure your windows, doors, and hatches are still well sealed. Mildew loves to grow in windowsills on boats (especially Grand Banks windowsills), so don't allow it to even start. Spritz the windowsills with a mildew spray cleaner and follow it up with Clorox bleach spray. This will kill the mildew and prevent it from coming back in the near future. You can also lay a strip of fabric (part of an old towel, for example) in the sill to soak up any condensation that might occur. If untreated, the mildew can grow in the area between the windows (where they meet in the middle), and the only way to reach that area to fully kill the mildew and clean it is to remove the windows.

Moss on a windowsill

Exterior Checklist

▶ **Wax on, wax off.** Wax is the best protectant for your boat. There are many benefits to a freshly waxed boat. Stains don't "soak in" to the gelcoat as easily; you can go longer between washes; water stains wash off easier; and, of course, your boat is protected from harmful UV rays. If your boat hasn't been waxed in a while, consider waxing it (or hiring a detailer to wax it) so you don't have to wash it as much over the winter. Or, if you had your whole boat waxed in spring, just wax the deck and abovedeck structures again before winter. By then, they will need it from all the sun and weather exposure they received from summer, and these areas take more of a beating from winter weather conditions as well. Waxing them again before winter will make it much easier to clean and maintain them come spring.

▶ **Prevent mildew from attacking your canvas.** Spritz the canvas with a mildew spray cleaner on a regular basis to help prevent mildew from setting in. Once the canvas looks as though it might be easier to mow than to scrub, you are too late in the fight against mildew. If you have a ski boat or an enclosed flybridge, make sure there is some sort of ventilation coming through the canvas, either with a mesh patch to let air in or simply by not tightening the canvas completely in one area. Even though the canvas cover will keep out the rain, it won't keep the air dry. The moist air that develops under the canvas cover can foster the growth of mildew, and even when warm days are forecast, without ventilation there is no way for the air to dry up enough to prevent the mildew from growing further. Have your local canvas maker add a few ventilation patches in your canvas cover, or leave a small section somewhat loose so air can flow through.

▶ **Bring in all exterior cushions.** I know they are labeled "weatherproof" or "water resistant," but that means only if a little rain gets on them. It doesn't mean they can withstand rain or other moisture for long periods of time. Mildew grows quickly in wet cushions, no matter what material they're made of, and if left for a long time, it can be difficult to remove. Consider that the longer a stain sits, the harder you'll have to scrub or the stronger the cleaner you'll have to use. Both break down the material you're trying to clean, which makes it harder to clean the next time. Such a vicious little circle cleaning can be!

▶ **Clean out clogged drains.** The next time you wash your boat, notice whether it's taking a while for any drains to clear or if any drains are outright clogged. If they're draining slowly now, they'll only get worse once the leaves start to fall (if your boat is near any trees) or from any other debris that falls onto your boat. Spray the hose directly into the drains at full pressure to make sure they're clear. If they still aren't draining, or if you can tell that something is in there, use a wire or narrow PVC tube to poke into the drain and try to push any debris through it.

▶ **Move outdoor deck carpets in.** As with canvas, any fabric that remains outside will surely grow mildew. Although it isn't the end of the world for those items, it will cause you a lot more work in spring when all you have to do right now is roll up the outdoor deck carpets and store them inside. Just think—if you move them inside now, you won't have to spend more than a minute dusting them off in spring!

▶ **Drive the spiders crazy.** Or better yet, drive them away. Spider droppings that sit on fabric, vinyl, or gelcoat for long periods of time can soak in and are hard to fully remove. Even heavy-duty rubbing compound doesn't always take out the stains. You'll always be left with a small tan circle to remind you that all you had to do was this one simple task: Go to your local hardware store and buy a plug-in ultrasonic spider repeller. Plug it into the flybridge or helm area of your boat (or someplace where it won't get wet from rain) and watch the spiders leave and know that

This ultrasonic device drives spiders crazy—and away.

they won't come back! These devices emit a super-high-pitched sound that interrupts their daily living (eating, mating, weaving webs) and prevents them from going anywhere near that area.

▶ **Don't leave the leaves.** As soon as leaves fall onto your boat, hose them off. You may have to do this several times until the tree near your boat has finished "falling." If left on the gelcoat, the leaves cause a brown stain once they get wet. If allowed to soak in (even on a waxed boat), the stains are hard to remove. It requires a lot of rubbing compound and some pretty strong UV rays to help bleach them out over time.

▶ **Don't let the dinghy get dingy.** If you've just brought the dinghy out of the water, clean it up while it's still wet. Algae, once dry, cause a brown stain on the hull that is difficult to remove. Spray the inflatable areas with Inflatable Boat Cleaner, let it sit, scrub it in with a soft bristled brush, and hose it off. To clean dried algae off the bottom, spray it with a rust remover spray (such as Rust SprayAway), use a soft hand brush to spread it around that area, and hose it off.

This might look like a lot of work at first, but if you can tackle these things over a few days, you'll be a lot happier next spring when you don't have to mow the grass out of the windowsills, scrape dried Coke and ketchup from the fridge, or paint the rest of the dinghy brown to match the dried algae stains on the bottom of it. A little prevention goes a long way!

Keep It Up or Let It Go

That seems to be the question many of us ask as we look at the mildew encroaching on our canvas bimini top or the spider droppings on our white vinyl seat cushions. Should I keep after those things on a regular basis, or is it all right to just let it go till later? Many of us just don't have the time at the beginning and end of each boating season or during the off months to keep on top of these things. Or maybe you have plenty of time, but cleaning your bilge just isn't on your list. I'm all for procrastination, so here are the boat detailing projects you should stay on top of and the ones you can save for later.

Wax It Away

The more often you wax your boat (at least twice per year), the more time you can let go in between washes; for example, instead of washing it every two or three weeks, you might be able to get away with every four or five weeks. Wax protects the gelcoat from harmful UV rays, as well as general wear and tear, scuff marks, and water stains. It prevents bird droppings from "soaking in" and helps prevent the gelcoat from oxidizing over time.

I always suggest to my customers that they wax their hull once a year and wax the decks and abovedeck structures twice each year, once in spring and once before winter. The decks and abovedeck structures get hit more directly with UV rays, as well as water stains and bird droppings, so these areas are the first to fade. Waxing them every six months will keep them looking good year-round.

If It's Yellow

Actually, no matter what color it is, don't let it mellow. Flush your tanks on a regular basis if they're used often, and definitely before you put the boat away for the winter. There is nothing worse than boarding your boat in spring for the first time only to be reminded by the smell of the heads of just how many parties you had on the boat the previous season. (Sorry to be so graphic, but that ought to make you run out and pump the tanks right now!)

Likewise, if there is anything damp inside the boat, such as cushions, towels, curtains, or other fabrics, take them out and clean them (throw them in the washing machine or get them dry cleaned), and make sure they're completely dry before putting them back in the boat (or store them in a dry storage place off the boat). This is definitely not something you want to let go!

Keep on top of carpet stains as they occur, simply because it's easier to remove a fresh stain than one that has thoroughly soaked into the carpet fibers. Use water and vinegar or products like Folex or an "oxy" cleaner to spot-clean. And it's a good idea to get the carpets professionally steam cleaned once a year to keep overall traffic areas from becoming too soiled. If you let your carpets go, eventually spot cleaning won't make a difference and in fact will actually make the carpets look worse. You'll have a few really clean spots while the rest of the carpet is slightly darker from being soiled by foot and paw traffic over time.

General interior cleaning is something you can let go until you need to spiff up the boat for a party or take it out for the first time in spring. The crumbs you left in the galley drawers or on the counter won't grow over winter into larger, more menacing crumbs. They'll be the same little crumbs they were at the end of the season and can easily be vacuumed up whenever you get a chance.

The Green Monster

Eventually, mildew will find your boat and attach itself to your lovely canvas, especially around the edges and zippers. You can let it go for a while, but you want to treat it and scrub it off before it turns into thicker, mosslike mildew or it will not only be much more difficult to remove, it will eventually weaken the integrity of the canvas from all the hard scrubbing it takes to remove it. The best way to prevent mildew from winning the race is to clean your canvas with boat soap and water and a mild scrub brush. Then, while it's wet, spritz it with mildew spray cleaner (Lysol or Tilex) or Mold Off (www.moldoff.org) and let it soak into the canvas. Mildew spray cleaners are effective for several weeks, helping keep mildew at bay without a lot of work on your part.

Although it's not green, rust is another stain that should be treated on a regular basis. Often I see rust stains dripping down the side of the boat from a stanchion or other metal object. If they haven't been there for a long time, I can easily remove them with a spray that removes rust from fiberglass (available at boat supply stores). And, of course, if you have a good coat of wax on your boat, the rust stain will sit on top of it and not eat into the gelcoat, provided you treat the stain every so often and keep that area waxed. However, it's best to treat the rust problem at the source. Find out why rust is developing in that area. Maybe something needs to be resealed or a metal screw or stanchion needs to be replaced. If left to sit for a long time, rust stains can be difficult to remove from gelcoat and might eventually need to be wet-sanded off and the area re-waxed.

Birds, Leaves, and Spiders

Those three things are probably what most frustrate boaters who try to keep their boat clean. If your boat has a good coat of wax, droppings and leaves can remain on the gelcoat without permanently staining it, but it's still better to get after these things as often as you can. If you don't have much time, keep a hose handy at your slip and simply hose off your boat every week or two. Even if you don't scrub away the stains, just getting the top layer of them sprayed off with a hose will allow the sun to bleach out the stain. The same thing goes for brown and purple leaf stains. Hose off the leaves and let the sun bleach out the stains; it will take only a day or two. But that's why you want a good coat of wax on your gelcoat. If the sun is strong enough to "remove" stains on the gelcoat, just think what it's doing to the gelcoat itself!

Washing your boat is something you can let go for a month or two if you have a good coat of wax on it or you moor it in a covered slip. Sure, there may be more water stains dripping down your gelcoat, but with a good coat of wax, they'll wipe or wash right off the next time you wash your boat. Without a good coat of wax, they will be more difficult to remove and will require more scrubbing, or you'll have to wax them off with a cleaner wax. It's a vicious circle—if you don't keep your boat waxed, you'll end up having to wax it just to get the stains out!

Water stains are a natural occurrence. The best way to remove them quickly (if you don't have time to wash your boat) is to spray them with vinegar or Simple Green and wipe them away with a rag. Don't use anything stronger than that; it will remove the wax in that area, which is most likely the area that needs wax the most because that's where the water stains accumulate. (Like I said, it's a vicious circle.)

The Hour-a-Week Boat-Cleaning Plan

If you have only an hour each week or want to spend only an hour each week maintaining the cleanliness and appearance of your boat, here is a short checklist of the tasks you should spend your time on.

1. When you arrive at your boat, stand on the dock and look it over as a whole. Anything amiss will catch your eye immediately, such as a panel of canvas flapping in the breeze (possibly marking the gelcoat each time the metal snap hits it) or possibly a ding in the gelcoat. Make a mental note to take care of these issues soon.

2. If you have more than an hour, plan to wash your boat. But assuming you don't, take out the hose and just hose down the decks. Don't get the rest of the boat wet or you will have just turned the light layer of dust on your boat into a light layer of mud and it will be even dirtier the next time you come down. Just hose the decks and make sure the drains aren't clogged with leaves or debris.

3. Your glass windows will be dusty, so grab a few microfiber rags and some window cleaner such as SprayWay or Plexus and spray and wipe them down. Your plastic and Lexan windows will also be dusty, so use a microfiber rag and a cleaner such as Meguiar's or Mer-maids Plastic Cleaner to spray and wipe down those windows or panels.

4. With your damp rags from cleaning the windows, provided they're not too dirty, wipe down the helm station area in the enclosed flybridge if you have one. A clean rag with either of the window sprays will also work well on the dash area.

5. Take a spray bottle of Simple Green, a bottle of cleaner wax, and a microfiber rag and walk around the exterior of the boat looking for water stains, scuff marks, and bird dropping stains. First try wiping them clean with just the rag and Simple Green. If they don't come out,

apply a small amount of cleaner wax, rub it in, and wipe it off. This is a good way to remove any marks and stains in between washes.

6. The interior of your boat shouldn't be too dirty if you cleaned it after each outing. Keep a small portable vacuum cleaner on the boat if you don't have a central vacuum system. This way, you can quickly vacuum around the edges of the floor, the countertops, and over the cushions to remove most of the crumbs and dirt. Then take a microfiber rag or a duster and simply dust all flat surfaces—counters, tables, ledges, the edge of bookcases, etc. Check the toilets while you're there and do a quick swish of the toilet brush if needed. Check the fridge to make sure nothing has leaked or dripped or is growing and staging a coup against you.

If you do these six tasks on a regular basis, even every other week, you're one big step ahead of ever having so much dirt, dust, and debris on your boat that it takes a full day to clean it. This, of course, assumes that you wax your boat at least once a year and wash it at least once a month if it's moored in an uncovered slip. A little care on a more regular basis will go further in the effort to keep your boat looking good and in good condition. It's not nearly as overwhelming as trying to do it all in one weekend, and it allows for a little more procrastination over time—something we can all enjoy!

Selling Your Boat

The day you decide to sell your boat will surely cause you to experience a wide range of emotions, but the emotion that will sneak up on you and surprise you the most is that of awe. You'll stand there on the aft deck looking into your boat and realize just how much stuff you have on and in your boat that you now have to get off your boat!

It was so easy for you or your spouse or your friends to bring that one bag of potato chips or that liter of soda pop or that box of crackers for the opening day parade you had in 1979, but it's all still on the boat! Along with all of the canned goods and Ziploc bags you stocked up on just in case that small marina you were stopping at didn't have those items.

The day has come when you must enter your floating storage unit and turn it back into a clean and spacious boat. It can be a daunting task, but if you divide the work over a week and invite everyone who ever brought a bag of potato chips or box of crackers onto your boat to help out, you'll get it done in no time!

Exterior Detailing

Your first task is to make the outside of the boat look good. This is where the first impression will be made, and if the first impression is made in the first five seconds, as they say, you want the gloss on your gelcoat to be what catches their eye, not the water stains or the green mildew growing along the windowsills.

Start by emptying out exterior lazarettes and storage compartments. First, take everything out of them and clean the inside. Ideally, the lazarettes and storage compartments should be empty and their contents removed from the boat or put in your dock box, but if you must keep some items in the exterior compartments, choose things that are useful or have a purpose there and fit neatly into the compartment.

After you've cleaned out the exterior compartments, it's time to wash the boat. Your scrub brush or sponge should touch every inch of the boat to make sure everything gets clean. Potential buyers will look under things, test things, and lift up every hatch on the boat. Once they buy the boat, they may never touch or notice these things again, but that doesn't matter. Everything needs to be clean for their first tug at the hatch. Spend some time in the flybridge or helm area and wipe the dashes clean, as well as the inside of the Isenglass or windows.

If your boat hasn't been waxed in a while or is starting to look more matte than glossy, consider waxing it to bring back the gloss. Obviously, the last thing you want to do when selling your boat is to spend more money on it. If you hire someone to wax it, have them wax only the decks and abovedeck structures, which are the main areas of the boat that potential buyers will see as they're walking up to or around the boat.

Clean up canvas and vinyl as best you can. If the cushions or canvas covers are in bad shape (green, wet, and mildewy), take them off the boat, clean them, and allow them to dry before putting them back on the boat or storing them elsewhere.

A few other exterior detailing tips:

▶ Clean fenders and power cords with acetone or inflatable boat cleaner and a Mr. Clean magic pad to get them spotless and looking as good as new.

▶ Bleach any mildewy lines with mildew spray cleaner.

▶ Pull up any exterior carpet that is in rain's way so it doesn't mildew over time. Leave any carpet in the covered flybridge or helm area. It looks nice and will protect the nonskid, but you'll need to check it every now and then and vacuum or shake it out.

▶ If the last time you took the boat out was that opening day parade in 1979 and your registration tabs show 1979 as the latest year, remove them!

▶ Make it easy to board your boat, whether that means turning it bow in or stern in depending on your dock configuration, or placing a step stool where needed.

Interior Cleaning

Cleaning the interior of your boat will make the exterior cleaning you just did seem like a breeze. (I didn't want to tell you this earlier.) Bring empty boxes, paper bags, plastic garbage bags, cleaning rags and paper towels, cleaning products (you probably already have them on your boat), and your favorite music.

Start by emptying out the cupboards, drawers, and storage compartments. Vacuum and clean them out well. You can put back a few useful or practical items if you must, but take as much as you can home with you. You'll have to remove these things from your boat eventually, so you might as well start now. Besides, your goal is to create a clean and spacious look. Better to let potential buyers see how spacious the storage compartments are rather than show them just how much stuff you can cram in there!

Polish wood walls, doors, and trim with an orange oil spray. This will give them an attractive sheen and help the boat smell good. Clean the head with a fresh-smelling cleaner like Pine-Sol and pour tank treatment into the toilet. An easy way to start cleaning the galley is to simply vacuum all the crumbs from the stove, stovetop, and drawers, then spray with a cleaner to remove any remaining marks, dirt, or stains.

Clean out the fridge well. Remove everything, then wipe it out, including storage bins and trays, and wipe out the freezer. You may want to defrost the freezer and keep it turned off and the door ajar. Either way, be sure to thoroughly dry the inside of the fridge and freezer (if you defrosted it) so that water doesn't cause any mildew to grow over time. Then put a box of baking soda in the fridge and another one in the freezer to keep these spaces fresh.

Setting the Stage

Staging is something real estate agents do well. This helps potential buyers visualize their dream. You can do the same type of staging with your boat. Once you've cleaned the interior and removed most or all of your personal items, you can bring select items back on the boat that will add to its ambi-

A nicely staged boat for sale

ance. Set the table for two with attractive, clean placemats, decorative plates, cloth napkins, and even a bottle of wine with two wineglasses.

Hang a decorative dish towel and matching oven mitt near the stove. Put a teapot on the stove with an attractive teacup and saucer on the counter. Put silk flowers on a table and a fresh towel in the berth with a good-smelling bar of soap on the sink. Lay a throw blanket over the bed with a book.

The goal with staging is to make the boat feel comfortable and inviting to help potential buyers imagine themselves having a nice meal with someone on their boat, making a warm cup of tea on a cold day, or curling up with a good book. But avoid the cluttered look, and make sure all items used for staging are clean and look new.

Take photos of your boat only after you've cleaned and staged it. Use a camera with a wide-angle lens so people can get a better idea of your boat's layout instead of showing tiny, cramped-looking rooms.

These suggestions will make your boat look better to potential buyers and be much easier to sell, whether you're selling it on your own or through a brokerage. If your boat hasn't sold in the first month after you've thoroughly cleaned it, you'll want to wash it at least once a month and check the interior each time you're aboard. If a lot of people have been viewing your boat, you may need to vacuum the interior, dust surface areas, and make sure the toilet is clean.

If you're selling your current boat to buy a bigger and better boat, just remember that bigger simply means more places to store bags of potato chips, boxes of crackers, and cleaning products. Tell your friends that if they board with one bag of chips, they have to leave with two.

Critter Prevention

There is no doubt about it that spiders and other insects love boats! And the closer your boat is moored to a shore, wetlands, or vegetation, the more insects and spiders your boat will attract. With all those juicy little insects come hungry little birds. Once they've eaten some of the insects, guess what comes with now full little birds? Yes, bird droppings. (And guess what comes with spiders? Spider droppings!) Then there are otters and muskrats that target your boat because your swim platform makes an excellent sunning deck for them, as well as a great place to rest and eat the crab they just caught. And your exhaust opening makes an excellent hideaway.

In the years that I've been detailing boats, I have come across interesting methods that boaters use to scare away critters. Most of these methods have scared only me (inflatable pythons and masks) or, thanks to my poor depth perception, have caused only me to trap myself in the owner's strategically placed fishing wire. Although annoying (because I'm usually the one having to clean up after these critters), I find it humorous when I see seventeen little sparrows sitting on the inflatable snake or surrounding the plastic owl perched on the hard top as if it were their fearless leader. Somehow these sparrows must inherently know that pythons, in their non-inflatable form, don't actually exist in North America.

This fake bird most likely won't scare off the real ones.

If it is true that acidic pigeon droppings can cause a steel bridge to deteriorate, imagine what similar bird or spider droppings can do to your gelcoat, vinyl, plastic windows, and canvas. It takes time for the acid in these droppings to do much damage, but if they're sitting on unprotected fabrics or gelcoat, they can slowly deteriorate that material. The following section lists each type of critter, the mess they can make, the damage they can do, how to clean up after them, and how to prevent them from taking over your boat.

Bird Droppings

The slight acidic content in all animal droppings can eat into the material they're sitting on if the droppings are not removed on a regular basis. Bird droppings are most annoying for making your boat's deck and abovedeck structures look like Picasso masterpieces with their colorful splotches, especially in fall when birds are eating berries. If you haven't waxed your gelcoat in a while (more than a year), bird droppings can actually "soak into" the porous gelcoat and become even more difficult to remove without using heavy-duty rubbing compound or chemical cleaners. Therefore, the first and foremost defense is to keep your boat waxed. Even if the inflatable Komodo dragon is scaring away the birds from landing on your rails, not much can stop those birds flying overhead from hitting your boat. If your gelcoat has wax on it, these stains will sit on top of the wax instead of the gelcoat itself.

One of the only bird deterrent systems I've seen work fairly well is stringing fishing wire near the rails and other areas where you don't want birds perching. Fishing wire is very thin yet somewhat reflective, so although birds can see that something is there, they're not able to focus on it and therefore don't feel safe landing in that area. You can also tie two-foot-long pieces of mylar flash tape (sold at hardware and household variety stores) on the rail every twelve inches or so in other areas where birds congregate. Choose silver flash tape if you can find it because the colored tapes can run onto gelcoat or metal if they get wet.

Mylar flash tape scares birds away from your railings.

If your boat has been covered with bird droppings, the first thing to do is give it a good soapy wash. Don't spend time at this point trying to scrub off the bird droppings. Your main goal is simply to remove the crusty top layer. After thoroughly rinsing, you'll still see a colorful mark where the bird dropping was, but now you can more easily remove the stain in one of two ways. You can remove it yourself, or you can let nature do the work, which means letting the sun bleach out the stain naturally. It takes only a few days and the stain will be gone or significantly lightened. If you want to remove the stain yourself, take some cleaner wax (such as 3M Cleaner Wax) and a microfiber rag and rub a small amount of the cleaner over the stain until it lightens or is gone completely. Then buff off the wax dust with another corner of the rag.

Spider Droppings

Those little black dots you see all over the white vinyl seats in your enclosed cockpit are spider droppings. Spiders love living in enclosed cockpits and flybridges because it's typically warmer in there and they have many good hiding places, as well as places to make their nests and birth their millions of babies. This is one critter you want to exterminate on a regular basis simply because they reproduce so rapidly and in such high numbers.

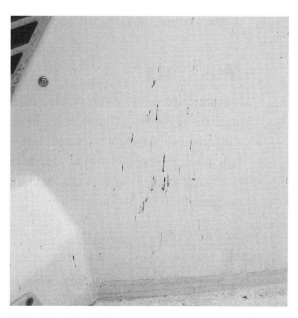

Spider dropping stains

First, remove their black dot droppings by spraying Simple Green on the vinyl over each black dot and let it sit for about 30 seconds. This will loosen the dropping and you'll easily be able to wipe it off with a rag. You can follow up by using 303 Aerospace Protectant on all of the vinyl to protect it from UV rays as well as prevent spider droppings from soaking in.

You can remove the spiders from your enclosed cockpit or flybridge area in one of two ways—with an ultrasonic pest control device or with an insect spray or a fogger. To be effective, an ultrasonic pest control device needs to be plugged into a receptacle in your enclosed cockpit area. The device works best when it's positioned close to where the spiders are actually living and nesting. It sends out an ultrasonic sound that people and dogs cannot hear. Spiders can hear it and it basically disrupts their lifestyle in that area, causing them to evacuate and find another place (that is, another boat) to live in. You will need to change the device about every three months because spiders eventually get used to a certain pitch and it will no longer be effective. Simply buy a different brand with a slightly different pitch.

If you're able to be off your boat for a full 24-hour period, you might consider fogging the enclosed area. Buy a fogger that specifically kills spiders and their eggs. Set the fogger in the middle of the enclosed area, push the trigger, and leave the area immediately. When you come back the next day, open as many windows or panels as you can to let fresh air in while you clean up after the fogger and vacuum up everything that dropped from the spiders' hiding places.

Muskrats

Muskrats aren't known for making messes on boats, but rather sinking them. They enter through your exhaust outlet and chew their way into the boat. They'll chew through anything, and the more they chew through, the more water is let into the hull, bilge, or engine room of your boat. The best way to prevent any critter from entering your boat underwater is to put metal mesh screens over all underwater openings.

Otters

Although cute, otters can make a huge, stinky mess on your boat with all of their discarded crab shells and droppings. They enjoy sunning themselves on swim platforms and eating their shellfish dinner there, too. If you come across this, just hose off the area where they've been, scrub it with soap and water, and rinse well. If there are stains on the nonskid or decking from their little shenanigans, you can remove them the same way you would remove bird droppings. Either let the sun bleach them out or remove them with rubbing compound. Make sure this area is waxed to prevent future stains from soaking in.

Some people rig up wire with an electric current passing through it to prevent otters from getting on their boat. If you can't do this at your slip (most marinas don't allow it), you may simply need to wash this area on a regular basis or as often as the otters are using your boat.

Diving Services

If a diver is coming to your boat to replace the zincs, check your propeller, or find your keys, it would also be a good time to have the diver clean the bottom of your boat. How often is enough?

If you moor your boat in fresh water, you should need to do this only when you have your zincs checked. If you moor your boat in an area with active marine growth (coral, barnacles, algae, and other such growth), you will need to have the bottom of your boat cleaned on a regular basis. How often depends on the type of marine growth in your area and how quickly it comes back once scrubbed off. If coral is an issue, it should be cleaned off every few weeks. The coral that accumulates on a boat bottom with poor or no antifouling paint can grow so large that it requires removal with a scraper instead of a steel wool pad. If a scraper is needed, it will take more time to do the job and therefore cost more money. The boat's performance can also become compromised due to coral fouling the hull, propellers, and engine water intakes and can cause the engine to overheat as well.

If you moor your boat in an area with less aggressive marine growth, you should have the bottom cleaned every four to five weeks year-round. These recommendations are for boat bottoms with bottom paint rated in fair to good condition. Boat bottoms and outdrives with poor or no paint should be cleaned every two to four weeks depending on the marine growth in your area. The goal is to clean the bottom on a regular basis so a scraper doesn't have to be used, thus degrading the remaining bottom paint or scratching the gelcoat. If the diver has to scrape off a considerable amount of marine growth each time he or she goes under your boat, too much time has elapsed between cleanings. Boat bottom cleaning should be scheduled more often to avoid excessive marine growth and loss of the boat's performance. Less drag can help increase boat speed and improve fuel efficiency.

While the diver is under your boat, have them clean all unpainted metal surfaces such as props, shafts, trim tabs, struts, rudders, engine intakes, and outdrives. You might also suggest that they check and clear all of the through-hulls, speedometer wheels, and depth sounder transducers.

Cruising with Your Non-Boating Friends

When the weatherman predicts sunny skies and warm temperatures for opening day weekend, all the people you promised a boat ride to at the office or on your brother's wife's side of the family will start coming forward, dropping hints about how nice it must be out on the lake this time of year. It doesn't matter than none of them has ever set foot on a boat. You will invite them and they will come and you will spend the whole cruise making sure they don't break or clog the head, fall off the boat, or get seasick on your new settee.

There are many ways you can make your non-boating friends feel safe and comfortable on your boat while at the same time allowing yourself a little freedom from constantly "babysitting" or giving instructions to your guests. Before they arrive, clean and organize your boat so it's easier for them to move around and to find things. Once they arrive, tell them what to expect once you're under way and how to use things on board. The following tips might help.

Clothing and Gear

Your friends have most likely seen many boat advertisements with a beautiful woman in a swimsuit sunning herself on the forward deck or a group of longtime friends enjoying a glass of wine on the aft deck, all wearing white pants, a pink button-down shirt, and a seafoam green argyle sweater tied over their shoulders.

Rarely do these polished advertisements show what it's really like when a squall suddenly takes over your blue sky and you have to wear your argyle sweater as a hat to keep your head warm and somewhat dry.

The best way to help your non-boating friends prepare for their cruise is to send them a written invitation that suggests some items they should bring for their own comfort. Let them know that the weather can change quickly and that even the slightest breeze, when you're out on the water, can feel much cooler than what they're used to on their west-facing sundeck at home. This list should include a warm sweater or jacket, sunglasses, and a light rain jacket. They should bring a versatile hat that can protect them from sun, rain, or cooler temperatures. If you have a few extra raincoats (or you can buy cheap plastic raincoats at the drugstore), pack them in a bag in case any of your guests needs one. Pack a few extra sweatshirts or hats if you have them as well. This will ensure that everyone is comfortable, even if they didn't pack the right gear for themselves.

Another important issue you'll need to tackle is encouraging your friends to wear the right footwear. Of course, you don't want them slipping around on the deck, but you especially don't want heel marks in your teak or black scuff marks all over your freshly washed nonskid. When it comes to footwear, it seems that most people would rather wear what looks best over what is most practical. It always amazes me to see people trying to board a boat at the boat show in high heels or their work boots! As a detailer, I want to run over to them and tell them just how much time I'm going to have to spend at 7 a.m. the next morning in freezing cold temperatures scrubbing as hard as I can to remove the black marks they're about to leave!

Tell your friends to wear flat-soled shoes with soles that are light colored or non-marking. Most people will give you a blank stare when you say "non-marking" because if that's not the very reason they bought that pair of shoes, they'll have no idea what you're talking about. If you have teak decks, your greatest enemy is a high-heeled shoe, whereas with nonskid your greatest enemy is grease marks. Plan a casual party so that ladies coming from the office or your buddies coming from Clem's Auto Lube will feel more comfortable changing into sneakers.

How Things Work

Your friends will board your boat and tell you that your kitchen is cute, will ask where the bathroom is, and will want to go upstairs so they can see the view from the second floor. Your guy buddies will want to help you with the ropes and bumpers, and your lady friends will want to check out all those cute little bedrooms. That's fine. Let them speak as they will. But before you set sail, you should give them a quick tour of the boat, pointing out the things they may need to find or use once you've left the dock.

The three most important things you'll want to point out are how to use the head, how to access fresh water, and how to safely move about the boat. The best way to provide directions on how to use the head is to have a small plaque with simple instructions engraved on it and post it in the head. If you gather your friends around the head and tell them how to use it, chances are they won't remember much of what you say because they'll feel so silly that you have to show them how a toilet works at their age. By having a plaque, they won't have to remember any details and can simply follow it step-by-step when they need it most. You will still find your head clogged with all sorts of random objects when you get back to the dock and your friends are long gone. You'll wonder what strange rituals went on while you were at the helm, and where did the plaque go?

Show your friends how to access fresh drinking water or where you keep the water bottles. Let them know what can and can't go down the drain and where the garbage can is. Keep extra garbage can liners and paper towels on the counters so, in case of spills or the garbage can fills up halfway through the cruise, people aren't forced to get creative or fend for themselves. (Trust me, the last thing you want is for your non-boater friends to "get creative"!) Show your guests how to turn lights on and off but *do not* show them where the panel is with all of the neat-looking switches. If this is your only way of turning lights on and off, have the lights turned on before they arrive. You do not want your engineering buddies playing with those switches! They will surely think they can re-wire them so you can get free cable TV when you turn on the bilge pump.

Moving Objects

Before your cruise is under way, show your guests the easiest ways to get about your boat, from the aft deck to the bow and up to the flybridge. It's easier to quickly demonstrate to your guests how to properly navigate stairways and ladders than it is to get blood out of teak. In your grand tour, point out handrails and places they may not want to venture if the water gets too choppy lest they get sprayed or lose their balance.

Provide rubber placemats and suctioned cup holders so they have a place to put their drinks and snacks; otherwise, you will be cleaning up crumbs from "the spill of '08" a year from now. This is another reason to leave the paper towels in plain view—in case that crab dip goes sailing off the table into their laps.

Many people are affected by seasickness, or at least think they are. It's often more of a psychological issue, but if you can help your friends feel comfortable before you leave the dock, everyone will have a better experience on the water. You may not want to bring up the subject lest you get everyone thinking about it, but you might consider leaving a few bowls of sugared ginger for your friends to snack on, subtly letting them know of its handy side benefit.

Put a small container in a cabinet (in the head or galley) with a label marked "motion sickness prevention—help yourself" and fill it with seasickness tabs and motion sickness wristbands. If any of your guests start to match the color of their seafoam green argyle sweater, encourage them to go outside and get some fresh air or lie down inside on the aft berth. If someone does get sick, assure them that most boaters have experienced this at one time or another and by the time they've gotten it all out of their system and they're simply praying for death, you'll be back at the dock and all of the moving about will be over.

By providing your non-boating friends with information that will make their boat ride as comfortable as possible, you'll be helping them enjoy their experience, and you'll ensure that they'll want another boat ride in the future when their friends from the Midwest are in town. Yep, you've done it now!

Resources

The products listed below are those we work with most often and suggest you try. They are a good basis from which to start in search of your own favorite products. Under each company name, I have listed the product name and its suggested use.

Mer-maid (www.mermaid.com)
- Mer-maids® Plastic Cleaner—for plastic windows and Lexan
- Mer-maids® Canvas and Vinyl Cleaner—for canvas and vinyl
- Mer-maids® Boat Wash with 2% Carnauba Wax—for boat washing
- Mer-maids® Serious Soap—for boat washing
- Mer-maids® Super Swabby Bilge Cleaner—for bilge and engine-room cleaning, grease stains

Mold-Off (www.moldoff.org)
- Mold-Off Mildew Cleaner—for cleaning mildew out of fabrics (canvas, vinyl, carpets, etc.)

Latitude 43 (www.lat43.com)
- Organic Boat Soap—for boat washing (best for boats on fresh water)

West Marine (www.westmarine.com)
- Rust StainsAway—for removing dried brown algae stains on gelcoat

Starbrite (www.starbrite.com)

▸ Premium Marine Polish with PTEF—for waxing a new boat with no oxidation (great for using by hand or in between wax jobs)

▸ Rust Stain Remover—for removing dried brown algae stains on gelcoat

▸ Instant Black Streak Remover—for removing black water stains on gelcoat

Meguiars (www.meguiars.com)

▸ Flagship Premium Marine Wax—for waxing a new or lightly oxidized boat, by hand or with a buffer

▸ One Step Cleaner Wax (#50)—for waxing a light- to medium-oxidized boat (best results when using a buffer)

3M (www.3m.com)

▸ Marine Cleaner and Wax—for waxing a medium- to heavily oxidized boat (best results when using a buffer)

▸ Scotchguard Marine Liquid Wax—for waxing a new boat with no oxidation (great for using by hand or in between wax jobs)

▸ Imperial Compound and Finishing Material—for using on its own as the first step in a two-step wax job (strictly to remove oxidation) or mixing with a cleaner wax when you need a more aggressive compound and wax mixture

303 (www.303products.com)

▸ Aerospace Protectant—for protecting vinyl, plastic windows, and rubber

Awlgrip (www.awlgrip.com)

▸ AwlWash—for washing a boat painted with AwlGrip

▸ AwlCare Polymer Sealer—as a sealant (in place of wax) on a boat painted with AwlGrip

Plexus (www.plexus.com)

▸ Plexus Plastic Polish—for cleaning and protecting plastic windows

Marykate

▸ Spray Away—good general-purpose spray cleaner (for exterior use only)

MDR

▶ Krazy Klean—good general-purpose spray cleaner (for exterior use only; great for cleaning up teak decks)

California Car Dusters (www.californiacardusters.com)

▶ California Water Blade—best squeegee we've ever used (buy the Original Standard 12-inch blade, with the purple handle)

Mr. Clean (www.mrclean.com)

▶ Mr. Clean Magic Eraser (Extra Power)—works the best and lasts the longest

Gardena

▶ Gardena trigger nozzle—lasts a long time, high quality, plastic (won't scratch the gelcoat if you drop it), pivotal head (prevents wrist fatigue), great spray (best nozzle by far!)

Makita (www.makita.com)

▶ 9227 Variable Speed Polisher—great for waxing boats that are medium- to heavily oxidized

New products are introduced to the market every year, so this list will change over time. Please visit my website at **www.DeckhandDetailing.com** to see my running list of up-to-date resources and product reviews. You can also e-mail me with any questions or product suggestions at **deckhanddetailing@hotmail.com**. I always enjoy hearing from fellow boaters about the products they've tried and love.

INDEX

ABOUT THE AUTHOR

Natalie Sears started her boat-detailing business, Deckhand Detailing, in Seattle in 1990. From this hands-on experience she learned how to properly clean and detail boats, from older, heavily oxidized sailboats to brand-new glossy megayachts. She took time off from the company to get a business degree at the University of Washington and became a marketing manager at Microsoft. After a few years in the corporate world, she was ready to get back to working on boats and started up her detailing company again in 2002. Although she didn't grow up on or around boats (in fact, she's scared of water), she is an entrepreneur at heart and developed a passion for working on them and taking care of them. When not working on a boat, Natalie can be found riding her horse or relaxing at her cabin in the mountains in eastern Washington.